GREENHOUSE GARDENING FOR NOVICES

The Ultimate Beginners' Manual to Learn Everything About Cultivating Vegetables, Herbs, and Fruits Year-Round in Any Kind of Greenhouse to Savor Your Food with Your Family.

© Copyright 2023 - All rights reserved.

The content contained within this book may not be reproduced, duplicated or transmitted without direct written permission from the author or the publisher. Under no circumstances will any blame or legal responsibility be held against the publisher, or author, for any damages, reparation, or monetary loss due to the information contained within this book. Either directly or indirectly.

Legal Notice:

This book is copyright protected. This book is only for personal use. You cannot amend, distribute, sell, use, quote or paraphrase any part, or the content within this book, without the consent of the author or publisher.

Disclaimer Notice:

Please note the information contained within this document is for educational and entertainment purposes only. All effort has been executed to present accurate, up to date, and reliable, complete information. No warranties of any kind are declared or implied. Readers acknowledge that the author is not engaging in the rendering of legal, financial, medical or professional advice. The content within this book has been derived from various sources. Please consult a licensed professional before attempting any techniques outlined in this book.

By reading this document, the reader agrees that under no circumstances is the author responsible for any losses, direct or indirect, which are incurred as a result of the use of information contained within this document, including, but not limited to, errors, omissions, or inaccuracies.

Table Of Contents

INTRODUCTION
- Gardening in Ancient Times
- Gardening in the Early Centuries (12th to 16th Century)
- The Greenhouse and Gardening in the 21st Century

CHAPTER 1: THE BASICS OF GREENHOUSE
- How Do Greenhouses Work?
- Uses and Benefits of Greenhouse Gardening

CHAPTER 2: BEFORE GETTING STARTED
- What Size to Buy
- Positioning Your Greenhouse
- Choosing the Best Floor
- Glass vs. Polycarbonate Panes

CHAPTER 3: TYPES OF GREENHOUSES

CHAPTER 4: GREENHOUSE PARAMETERS
- Location
- Floor
- Foundation

CHAPTER 5: BEST GREENHOUSE EQUIPMENT AND ACCESSORIES
- Best Greenhouse Equipment You Need
- Basic Greenhouse Equipment
- Furniture to Store Your Greenhouse Equipment and Plants
- Greenhouse Irrigation and Drainage
- Greenhouse Lighting
- Climate Control and Heating Greenhouse Equipment
- Ventilation Equipment for Your Greenhouse
- Pest Control Equipment
- Soil Sterilizers
- Gardening Sieve – Sowing Sieve
- Plant Support Equipment

CHAPTER 6: SEED STARTING
- Hardening Off
- Sorting Your Seed Packets

CHAPTER 7: HOW TO GROW A GARDEN IN GREENHOUSE

CHAPTER 8: GROWING VEGETABLES, HERBS, AND FRUITS
- Herbs
- Vegetables
- Fruits

CHAPTER 9: HEALTH BENEFITS OF GROWING IN YOUR GREENHOUSE
- Improves Your Well-Being

    Can Help You Save Some Money
    Help The Environment
    Raise Your Quality in Life

CHAPTER 10: GREENHOUSE HACKS

CHAPTER 11: GREENHOUSE IRRIGATION SYSTEMS

    Overhead Misters
    Mat Irrigation
    Drip Tubing

CHAPTER 12: TEMPERATURE AND HUMIDITY FOR A GREENHOUSE

    Shade Cloth and Paint
    Air Flow
    Choosing an Exhaust Fan

CHAPTER 13: COMBAT DISEASE AND PEST

    Remove Bugs and Pests
    Provide Shade and More Sun
    Heating and Ventilation Problems
    Weed Control
    Weed Management
    Sources of Weed Seeds

CHAPTER 14: MISTAKES TO AVOID

    Not Doing Your Research
    Growing Too Much at Once
    Planting Seeds Too Close Together
    Not Checking for Pests or Cleaning for Disease

CONCLUSION

Introduction

Before we begin exploring what greenhouse gardening is all about; it is important for you first to know a little history behind the building, which we now call the greenhouse. You will read about some of the major developments in agriculture and backyard farming that eventually led to the use of heat, humidity, and sunlight penetration in a controlled area for forced planting. Now, you do not need to worry. This brief history lesson will not be full of technical terms or strange-sounding jargon. Relax, enjoy reading about the history of the greenhouse, and how gardening in such an enclosed place came to be.

Gardening in Ancient Times

Our story begins with one of the oldest known countries in the world, Egypt. When people hear the name Egypt, the first thing they usually think of is the Great Pyramid at Giza, or perhaps the legendary Sphinx and its riddles. They might also think of the pharaohs, the great kings and champions of Egypt; others might remember the boy king, who was named Tutankhamen. However, aside from its great pyramids and its plethora of gods and goddesses, Egypt has another contribution to the world's shared culture.

Around 4000 B.C., the Egyptians mastered the planting and harvesting of grapes. There are tomb drawings and hieroglyphs (ancient Egyptian writing) that show Egyptian farmers in the act of cutting grapes from vines, or sowing grape seeds in the soil. The Egyptians, like many nations around the world, knew that settled communities had to have a reliable source of food. No community, large or small, could hunt all the prey in the wild without bringing about a great disaster. So, all around the world, nations turned to the earth, wind, rain, and sun for the miracle of plant life.

The Egyptians were just one of the countries that figured out how to use seeds and plants as a food source. In China, some of the great scholars of the emperor prescribed certain ceremonies for sowing and planting seeds. This is reminiscent of tribal practices, like the dance of the Native American Indians during a good harvest.

On another distant shore, the Greeks were marveling at the life that sprouted from the ground. Their philosophers began asking questions about the origin and meaning of life. The natural sciences soon began to take hold in Greece. Around 300 B.C., Plato mentioned a few vague hints about "protected cultivation" in some of his writings. Later, during the same period, another intellectual, by the name of Theophrastus, observed that plots with manure mixed in them seemed riper and richer than those that had none. Theophrastus also mentioned that the ripened soil appeared to make the crops grow faster and healthier.

In Italy, many inventions were taking the country by storm. A man named Sergius Orata discovered how to make a heating system that passed heat through flues or vents in the floor. Other notable Italians like Columella and Pliny wrote about the use of different materials to protect young plants from harsh sunlight, excessive wind, and flood. During 100 to 380 A.D., the Italians were slowly learning how to manipulate the environment of plants to ensure their safety and fruitfulness.

Gardening in the Early Centuries (12th to 16th Century)

During the time of the Crusades, the Crusaders themselves helped spread a variety of plants by carrying them from their place of origin to foreign soil. Of course, for people who had never seen orchids or strange-shaped plants and herbs, these exotic treasures had to be replicated for the entire nation to enjoy. This started the plant trade and the endeavors of gardeners all around the world to successfully grow beautiful plants even though they were not suited to the country's climate.

In 1385 a story about flowers being grown in a glass pavilion in France captivated many gardeners. They, too, wanted to know what the glass pavilion was for, and whether or not they would be able to have their own. The story goes that the pavilion was built facing the south of France, for the plants to better catch the warm breeze during the day, and to be shielded from harsh wind as well.

Finally, during the Renaissance, reports of sheds with heating vents in them became the new standard for the middle class. During the 16th century, the green glass industry in Italy flourished. In the year 1550, the first botanical garden with a greenhouse was built at Padua.

The Greenhouse and Gardening in the 21st Century

The idea of having a place in which plants and flowers can bloom all year-round is a gardener's vision of paradise. Thus, when the glass industry boomed, and the idea for using better soil as well as heat manipulation for planting first came about in earlier centuries, the destiny of the greenhouse was already cast in stone. For many gardeners, having their own greenhouses right across their homes is indeed a dream come true. Instead of having to wait for the seasons to change, or for winter to pass, the gardeners can cultivate different kinds of fauna in the same enclosed space.

Today, with the rise of organic gardening, aquaponics, and other agriculture or aquaculture-related practices, the greenhouse stands at its prime. More and more individuals have returned to the basic necessities so highly valued by our ancestors: good food, and a healthy relationship with the earth, and elements that give birth to our sustenance.

So, you see, engaging in greenhouse gardening is not only about having a separate space in which to grow rare plants. It is also about connecting with nature on a deeper level and engaging in an activity so rewarding; you will never want to stop. The practice of greenhouse gardening offers many opportunities to anyone with a budding green thumb.

CHAPTER 1:

The Basics Of Greenhouse

Reenhouses are commonly known by alternate names such as glasshouses and hothouses. These are structures built to control the climate and such factors for growing plants. The structure of the greenhouse is made up entirely using glass and is extensively used to cultivate various plants.

The main point of setting up a greenhouse is to help in gardening during the winter months when there is insufficient sunlight for the plants. The controlled atmosphere, with sufficient heat and light, helps in solving a lot of issues, which are usually faced during the colder months. The main purpose of setting up the greenhouse is to gain optimal conditions, which will promote better growth.

In simpler terms, greenhouses are essentially buildings in which crops and plants are cultivated. Greenhouses extensively serve as substitutes for the natural living conditions for exotic plants. Greenhouses today also are built for aesthetic purposes, and large ones are used as visiting spots for tourists.

Greenhouses have enabled man to understand the plants he or she wants to cultivate and have thrown light on how to make use of this. Greenhouses are much more than just glasshouses. With an increase in population these days, lands are constantly being occupied by rapid urbanization, and often, there isn't much room for the crops to grow. Also, greenhouses are attributed towards reducing the cost of shipping and transporting the crops that are grown in suitable climates to other regions where the demand for that particular crop is met. They are used by countries everywhere to increase the number of crops to meet the needs of the population.

Greenhouses also extensively protect the plants that are being cultivated to be pest-free. Greenhouses attribute to protecting certain plant species that are used for research like medicinal plants and are studied to create more yields. They are also used to protect plant species that are on the verge of extinction. Since controlling the environment inside a greenhouse is a lot easier than controlling the temperature outside, greenhouses have attributed to a positive development in the field of cultivation, biology, and other forms of plant study.

The advent of the greenhouse has moved science and technology in the field of cultivation, farming, and gardening. It has today enabled affluent farmers to be able to grow crops that are usually affected by the weather changes. The basic idea of greenhouses has existed for a long time. The point was to somehow grow vegetables, fruits, or any type of plant even when the climate was not suitable for it. It was vital to find a way to somehow control the environment in which these plants were grown so that they get all the required nutrition. Thus, they slowly worked up the greenhouses that we have now.

How Do Greenhouses Work?

You might remember from grade school science class that plants need five things to grow. They are namely, light, optimal temperature, water, air, and nutrients. Greenhouses are constructed in a way to accommodate the first three needs. The rest of the variables depend on how often you water the plants and the type of soil and fertilizers you use.

How do greenhouses provide sufficient light and heat? To put it simple, these strategic structures trap these elements inside to create the perfect environment for plants. Here is a closer look at how that happens:

Step 1: Sunlight Enters the Greenhouse

Typically, greenhouses are made of clear plastic or glass. The translucent surface allows the sunlight to pass through and enter the greenhouse easily. It's essential to select a material that provides greenhouse plants with maximum sunlight access throughout the year.

Step 2: Heat Gets Absorbed

When the sunlight enters the structure, it gets absorbed into the atmosphere. Everything from the plants to the ground absorbs the light. The light is then converted into thermal energy (i.e., heat) during this process.

Step 3: Greenhouses Trap the Heat

Greenhouses are constructed to reduce the flow of thermal energy that travels outside the structure. The conversion of light makes this goal possible since the changed energy (or rather wavelength) makes it harder for the heat to escape.

Step 4: The Greenhouses Becomes Warm

The trapped heat warms the atmosphere (or air) inside the greenhouse structure. The air-tight construction of this structure ensures that the warmer air does not leave the building. Ultimately, its presence causes the temperature to rise, too, making it warm and toasty for the plants.

Step 5: The Temperature Stays Consistent

When sufficient light passes through the structure, the temperature inside the greenhouse gets warmed than the outdoor temperature. You might have to ventilate the building on hotter days during the summer. Otherwise, you risk exposing delicate plants to abnormal amounts of heat and light.

Alternatively, the greenhouse gets warm more slowly on shay or rainy days. That is why it works best in areas that get lots of sunshine.

The overall reduction of thermal energy flow and rising temperatures keep the atmosphere inside consistent temperatures for continuous periods.

You might wonder how all this helps the plants grow better. The key lies in the photosynthesis process. Greenhouse plans receive the optimal amount of sunlight and heat required for this natural process to occur. Their leaves (aka the food factories for plants) absorb a sufficient amount of heat and light. Then mix it with air in the atmosphere and water drawn out from their roots. Without going into scientific details, the combination of these elements activates a chemical reaction that forms simple sugars. These sugars are the plant´s food.

As a result, continuous sunlight and heat promote plant growth and development. The significant difference between outdoor and indoor temperatures makes it possible for gardeners to grow tropical plants, often found in warmer climates.

Uses and Benefits of Greenhouse Gardening

Whether gardening is your hobby or profession, building a greenhouse can take your efforts to the next level. It can also save you from the drastic consequences caused by unpredictable weather.

The primary purpose of greenhouse gardening is to protect crops from extreme weather conditions (both in the summer and winter) and pesky pests. The glasshouse shields it from environmental elements to promote the healthy growth of all types of plants, including ones you won't necessarily find in your region.

Here's a closer look at all the reasons why you should build a greenhouse:

1. **Optimum Planting**

Unpredictable can wash away or flood your backyard overnight. Even if the consequences are not severe, continuous storms and fluctuating temperatures can have a negative impact on plant growth. Without proper intervention, it can lead to ruined vegetable patches and rotten fruits.

Fortunately, a greenhouse can save you from potential heartbreaks and ruined crops. These weather-proof structures evade unfavorable seasonal changes by regulating the internal environment. Consistent temperature and humidity ensure that your plants grow without disruptions.

Consequently, your gardening efforts are no longer dependent on the natural environment. Eliminating this connection paves the way for versatility, and experimentation. Hobbyists and professionals can use greenhouses to adopt new gardening styles and diversify their planting options.

2. **You Get to Grow More Plants**

Greenhouses create sufficient insulation and heat for warm-season plants to survive regardless of their location. They are also more humid and warmer than the natural outdoor environment. These factors make the hothouses excellent choices for growing tropical plants (i.e., cranberry hibiscus, bananas, ginger, pineapple, papaya, and more) in colder regions.

What's more? There are no hard and fast rules about the type of plants you need to grow inside a glasshouse. The flexibility allows you to create the glass structure into a multipurpose gardening zone. The possibilities are endless here.

Some gardeners switch things by growing indoor and outdoor plant varieties under one roof. You can also use a mix of potted plants and plants directly grown on your soil, depending on individual gardening requirements.

If you plan things strategically, you can designate a section for fruits, vegetables, herbs, tobacco plants, and much more. The variety itself will make you feel giddy with excitement as you undertake an exceptional range of planting projects.

3. **Enjoy a Year-Round Harvest**

Gardeners have to follow a strict schedule when they are gardening in the open. Many plants have specific harvest cycles that you need to maintain dutifully. The stakes are higher for seasonal plants. All this can take a toll on you and also make it more challenging to get a good harvest each year.

Greenhouses lift off these restrictions by extending the growing season. With its assistance, you can grow plants a few weeks (and sometimes months) longer than expected. All thanks to its well-regulated and weather-proof environment.

4. **Keep Pesky Pests Away**

Like any grassy area, backyards are open invitations for pests, critters, and animals lingering around the neighborhood. These trespassers have no qualms about biting into your juicing fruits and veggies or walking all over the vegetable patch, squashing everything in their wake.

Worse than one-time invaders are the pests that start living inside your yard. These critters can become difficult to detect when they first drop by. They can also breed and multiply within weeks. These variables make it impossible for you to manage pests without causing problems for your beautiful garden.

Plus, most pest prevention techniques are invasive or toxic. Frequent usage can affect plant growth and trigger unwanted plant diseases.

You can prevent this from happening by building a greenhouse for your garden. The sturdy structure will function as an extra barrier against unwanted pests and critters. It also minimizes the use of toxic pesticides in the long-run.

5. **Cost-Effective Investment**

If you think greenhouses are costly investments, we have news for you. These hothouses are so much more than a 'gardening accessory.' Not only do greenhouses save your plants, but they prevent unwanted gardening expenses too. Imagine how much maintenance costs and repair fees you will have to pay without this protection. When you think about it, these advantages reduce your gardening budget too.

Greenhouses also generate greater yields for seasonal and non-seasonal fruit. The increase in production rates means more revenue for your small-scale gardening business. If you do not sell your fruits and vegetables, you still save a lot by skipping grocery runs for fresh produce.

In addition to this, greenhouses are multifunctional. They have enough storage space for your gardening tools. These might include small items like shovels, shears, and spare pots to bigger tools such as lawnmowers. Having a greenhouse eliminates the need to manage additional expenses required for building or expanding a garden shed.

You also save storage space in your garages and basements.

CHAPTER 2:

Before Getting Started

Here are a lot of considerations to be made before you get started a greenhouse. Obviously, there is a budget, but other factors may well influence your budget. If you live in a particularly cold area, then double glazing and heating are important, but in a hotter area, the primary considerations would be airflow and ventilation.

What Size to Buy

Bigger is not always best, but many people aspire to a large greenhouse. What size to buy will depend on the space you have available plus what you are planning to grow. Of course, no matter what size you buy, when you start to use it, you will run out of space and wish you'd bought a bigger one!

If you are buying a second-hand greenhouse or picking one up for free, then you have less choice in size and will usually make do with whatever comes up.

The most common size is 8x6-inch though you can get slightly smaller ones and very much larger ones. This is a good starter size, but you need to be aware that your space is limited, and you will struggle to fit a lot in. However, it is a great size for starting off seeds and growing a few tomatoes or chili plants.

Check any local planning or zoning regulations before you buy a greenhouse. If you are on an allotment, then check their rules too. The last thing you want is to put up your new greenhouse only to find you have breached a rule and then have to take it down. On allotments, you often need written permission for a greenhouse and to position it in a certain way. As to HOA's, their rules are anyone's guess, so check and be certain.

We would recommend visiting a shop that sells greenhouses and walking into a few different sizes. It will help you to visualize the space better and work out which one is best for you. Just remember to avoid the salesperson's charm, or you may end up with a very expensive greenhouse!

When looking for a greenhouse, you need to consider how easy it is for you to maintain and use the greenhouse. If your greenhouse takes a lot of time to maintain each year, then it means less time doing other jobs.

Positioning Your Greenhouse

Where you will put your greenhouse can influence the size, as well as other factors. Obviously, you need to position it, so it gets good sun throughout the day.

Avoid the north-facing slopes as the amount of light will not be sufficient. Do not build your greenhouse at the bottom of a slope, as it is likely to be the location of a frost pocket, meaning cold air will gather around your greenhouse. This makes your greenhouse colder, requiring more heating and reducing the benefits you get from your greenhouse.

If you have no choice but to site your greenhouse facing north, which is still better than not having a greenhouse at all!

Depending on your preference, you may choose to align your greenhouse in one of two ways.

Firstly, you can align it, so the sun tracks down one side of the greenhouse. The advantage of this is that one side gets lots of sunlight and the other gets less, allowing you to grow plants that require less sun or need a bit of shade on the side of the greenhouse furthest from the sun.

Alternatively, you can align your greenhouse, so the sun shines on one of the small ends, so the whole greenhouse gets sun throughout the day.

Which you choose is up to you, and it may be that the locations available to you in your vegetable plot influence the alignment.

As an 8x6-inch greenhouse is virtually square, the alignment to the sun is not so important. For larger greenhouses, it does become more important to ensure you maximize the sun for your plants.

Something else to consider is the direction of the prevailing wind in your area. Typically, you will position the door away from the wind. This helps secure your greenhouse and makes it a little less susceptible to wind damage.

You want to position your greenhouse where it is not under trees. Should the trees lose branches, then it will damage or even destroy your greenhouse.

Ideally, you want your greenhouse located in a sheltered spot where it is not going to be subjected to high winds. It may not always be possible, but if you can do this, then it will help prevent damage in the future.

If you are planning on using an irrigation system or installing electricity, then your choice of the site needs to take this into consideration. It needs to be somewhere that you can supply these services to without too much work or expense. If not, then you are stuck watering by hand and using paraffin or solar heaters like most gardeners!

Choosing the Best Floor

All of these decisions need making before you buy your greenhouse, and this is probably one of the most controversial!

Which floor you choose will depend a lot on what you are planning on growing in your greenhouse and your environment.

Your choices are:

- No floor, just use the soil.
- The concrete path down the middle, soil to either side.
- The concrete path down the middle, weed membrane on either side.
- Complete concrete floor.

They all have their pros and cons, but it is a personal decision based on your site, budget, and available resources.

The problem with this is that the weed membrane does not extend outside of the greenhouse, meaning the hard-to-reach edges become infested with weeds. This is okay on the left-hand side, but the right-hand side has been staged in place, so it is extremely hard to weed.

The lesson has been learned, and on my next greenhouse, the inside will be much more weed-proof! But back to choosing the best floor for your greenhouse.

The first option is by far the easiest because you don't need to do anything.

The downside of this is the weeds will love the heat in the greenhouse and will thrive. You will have a lot of weeding to do, and this can be very awkward to do when the plants are fully grown.

Some people do grow directly into the soil using bottomless pots. Just be aware that although this option is cheap, you will be battling weeds inside your greenhouse as well as outside.

You also run the risk of introducing soil-borne pests and diseases if you do not change the topsoil in your greenhouse every year or 2.

Having a paved path down the middle of your greenhouse is great as it helps with access and isn't too expensive. You can leave the soil bare on either side or cover it with a weed membrane.

This method works well, as when you put staging in your greenhouse, it becomes very hard to weed underneath it.

Putting weed membrane down will be effective in keeping the weeds away, providing you use a decent quality membrane. Expect to replace it every 2 to 5 years, depending on what you use, as it will perish and eventually allow weeds through.

The final option is by far the best but is also the most expensive as you have to buy paving slabs for the whole greenhouse or poured concrete.

With a larger greenhouse, this can soon become expensive. It is also more work as you have to lay sand and hardcore as well as level the paving.

The advantage of this is that it is a low-maintenance solution. When done properly with a weed membrane under the sand, you should get years of a weed-free greenhouse.

As everything will be in pots, you can also move your plants around so you can reposition them as necessary to get them more or less sun as required.

Glass vs. Polycarbonate Panes

Again, this is a personal preference, and both types of panels have their good and bad points. Glass is the more expensive solution, and the most fragile, panels can get broken by accident or vandals and need replacing.

However, glass technology is quite advanced, and you can get some great thermally insulated glass which is ideal for colder areas or heated greenhouses.

Most greenhouses use horticultural glass, which typically comes in 2-inch square panels, so you can end up with overlapping panels. The disadvantage of this type of glass is that it breaks easily into very jagged and sharp pieces. Because of the size, the panels come in, you overlap them, and over time this can become dirty and grow algae, which looks unsightly.

You can buy specially toughened glass for your greenhouse, meaning it isn't going to shatter from a simple touch. It is still breakable, but it will survive an impact from a football though a more solid ball will break it. Just be careful of the edges of toughened glass as that is its weak point. When handling this, make sure you never let the edges touch a rough surface.

Plastic or polycarbonate panels are much cheaper to buy and, for most applications, just as good as glass. The big advantage is that they are a lot harder break which is important if you have kids as accidents do happen.

Because the polycarbonate panels are much lighter than glass, they are also more susceptible to wind damage. In high winds, they can flex and pop out of the frame!

Glass is much heavier and gives your greenhouse a more rigid structure, something that is lacking with polycarbonate panels.

Many polycarbonate panels are slightly opaque, meaning you cannot see in or out clearly. It may not bother you, but some people don't like it, and it can reduce the amount of sunlight your plants get.

You should also be aware that most polycarbonate panels are twin-walled, meaning there are two sheets of plastic with an air gap in the middle. Over time water seeps into this gap, and algae forms, which you cannot remove. It has an impact on how much light gets into your greenhouse and also looks untidy. Surprisingly, polycarbonate can cost even more than toughened glass!

Both are easy to get your hands on, being available in many glaziers. Our personal preference is the plastic panels purely from the point of view that they are harder to break and less likely to smash if people throw stones at them.

CHAPTER 3:

Types Of Greenhouses

Here are several types of greenhouses, and their classifications are based on several factors.

There are greenhouses that are classified by the materials that are used, greenhouses classified in accordance to technology, and many other classifications. In this guide, we look at the broad types of greenhouses.

Low-Technology Greenhouses

Low-technology greenhouses are extensively used because of their tiny structures. They are typically three meters in height and have very little ventilation. They are the most inexpensive forms of greenhouses. These are typically used by small farmers and households to protect their plants. They provide facilities like warmer temperature, reduction in pests, and so on. They use very little technology and hence are easy to set up. These are most prominently found in places like Australia. The major problem with this kind is the lack of scope to optimize production due to low levels of technology. These types of greenhouses are usually dome structured.

Medium Technology Greenhouses

Medium-level greenhouses are those that have a distinct division between the wall and floor. They aren't very big and are usually about 5.5 meters tall. They have better ventilation facilities and use medium levels of technology. Medium-level greenhouses have glass walls or double plastic walls and are slightly more expensive than low-technology greenhouses. These kinds of greenhouses are able to generate higher yields and have good usage of water. They eradicate disease-causing pests. However, the major problem with this kind of greenhouse is the lack of temperature regulation. Another issue is that the greenhouse does little to optimize production.

High-Technology Greenhouses

High-level greenhouses are those that make use of high levels of technology. They are generally a lot taller and are about 8 meters high. These greenhouses optimize production. They have both wall and roof ventilation. With these greenhouses, temperature control is easy and can be regulated to suit crop needs. They are expensive. These greenhouses reduce the number of pesticides used and at the same time eradicate pests much more than other greenhouses. The products produced by the plants grown in high-technology greenhouses are fresh and of superior quality.

High Tunnel Greenhouse

High tunnels greenhouses are most commonly referred to as hoop greenhouses. They are usually made up of polyethylene fabric or a greenhouse film. They are very simple and are considered to be economically viable. This type of greenhouse allows the person to grow plants, and these plants have optimum produce and prolong the growing season of the plant. They are extensively used in Europe and the Middle East. They are usually used as temporary filaments and use low levels of technology.

Industrial Greenhouse

Industrial greenhouses are highly technological-driven greenhouses that are extensively used for commercial purposes. They cover vast areas of the land and are associated with industrial-scale production. They are extremely expensive and specific in nature. They come with several facilities, including huge amounts of vents, sunlight filters, and irrigation facilities, and so on. They are extensively used in companies that produce huge amounts of flowers for decorative purposes, farming companies, and so on. With this type of greenhouse, temperature control is very easy as the temperature can shuttle between cold and hot. This type optimizes production and yield and reduces pests by a huge amount.

Rooftop Greenhouse

Rooftop greenhouses are medium-level technological greenhouses that are specifically suited to urban areas where the problem of space arises. This type of greenhouse is largely ventilated, providing enough sunlight and good temperature conditions for the person. The plants usually have a larger yield. This type of greenhouse blends the usage of natural sources as well as manmade sources. For instance, the original greenhouse keeps the plants warm during the day and cold during the night, this is a fluctuation that can cause damage to the plants. Rooftop greenhouses prevent this due to the existence of a thermal mass.

Commercial Greenhouse

Commercial greenhouses are not used by amateurs and are professional greenhouses built to suit the needs of commercial industries. They are very expensive and have customizable features. They are specially designed, keeping the needs of the company. Thus, they are highly technology-driven and have several features like irrigation facilities, seed dispersion, storage, sunlight filters, and so on. They provide the most optimum production and eradicate pests.

Heated Greenhouse

Heated greenhouses have high levels of technology and are usually expensive. They are specific in nature because they cater only to the plants that grow in the summer but need to be cultivated in the winter. Heated greenhouses are extensively used on professional levels as well as in the amateur levels. There are several subdivisions in this type of greenhouse. They provide optimum production and have large vents, and many at times contain valves that can regulate the heat generated in the greenhouses.

Insulated Greenhouse

Insulated greenhouses are extensively used in areas where there are erratic climatic conditions. With these types of greenhouses, the temperature can be controlled and regulated to allow the plants to grow at their speed without the hindrance of spells of showers, heat, and other climatic fluctuations. These are extensively used by wealthier farmers, for they are extremely expensive and require a large investment. These types of greenhouses are also the type that makes use of high-level technology.

Modular Greenhouse

Modular greenhouses are specially designed to provide a platform to grow multiple crops in a small storage space. They are used by gardeners and farmers who want to expand their production but often can't because of limited space. Modular greenhouses have several shelves and occupy less space. They also have several pockets and layers to grow plants on. They are mainly technologically driven and are expensive. These types of greenhouses have perforations in their layers to allow the sunlight to go to the bottom layer and so on. Though they are pricey, they reduce the overall cost because they enable people to expand plant growth without having to invest in another greenhouse.

CHAPTER 4:

Greenhouse Parameters

Location

He location of your greenhouse also depends on many factors. The first factor is the type of plant you want to grow inside your greenhouse.

Tropical plants need maximum sunlight exposure, so you must choose a greenhouse where sunlight comes in an appropriate amount. Most houseplants and flowers need good exposure to sunlight but not direct.

Your location also depends on the climate of your area. If you live in a warm place, then you must need proper shading for your greenhouse.

However, if you live in a cold area, then you need maximum exposure to sunlight. Remember that the sun changes its position in different seasons.

A very sunny spot in June should not get any sun exposure during the January season, and you must consider this fact before choosing your greenhouse location.

Floor

You have a choice of what kind of floor or base you want for your greenhouse. Many people don't bother to cover their greenhouse base, and they generally have mud or another floor where they constructed their greenhouse. This gives a natural look to your greenhouse. But it is not advisable to keep your floor open because many insects, worms, and rodents may grow inside the mud and should harm your plants. Some base constructions are available with the greenhouse construction kit, and you don't need to buy extra material for your base. But if it is not available in your kit, you can buy it from the market. Concrete floors are a good option for your greenhouse's base as they make the best place to put your benches and other materials. Sometimes, wooden floors are also good for your greenhouse

Foundation

When you are building a greenhouse, the first step is to build a foundation. This needs to be done properly for you to have a solid greenhouse that will stand the test of time.

Whatever you decide to make your foundation out of, it needs to be both level and square. It needs to be big enough for the outside dimensions of the greenhouse to ensure it fits properly and can be secured. You can buy pre-made greenhouse bases, and these are worth considering, but just be aware that these still need a flat and level surface to be installed on and will still need a foundation beneath them.

When building your greenhouse base, you can either make it out of poured concrete, or you can use sand and paving stones. Both are suitable and do the job well, though the latter has the advantage of being moveable in the future if necessary.

Ensure that not only are the edges of your base square but also that the diagonal measurements between the corners are also identical.

Under the base, you will need the foundation which is what supports the weight of the greenhouse, which is secured to and prevents damage in windy weather.

If you live in an area where the ground freezes, then your greenhouse foundation needs to be below the frost line. This is to prevent damage to your structure from the ground heaving as it freezes and melts. Your local Building Permit Agency will be able to tell you where the frost line is in your area. In warmer areas, this is only going to be a couple of inches at most, but in the colder, northern areas, it can be as much as a few feet.

One good way of insulating your foundation and protecting it is to use 1-inch foam insulation. Put this down to your frost line to reduce heat loss through the soil, which has the benefit of reducing your heating costs.

The foundation is essential because this is what you are securing your greenhouse too. It will prevent weather damage and warping in hot or cold weather. If you do not secure your greenhouse properly, then don't expect it to last the growing season. If the greenhouse starts to warp, then you can find your panes shatter or crack and become very hard to re-fit. You can also find doors and windows become stiff and very difficult to use too.

If you have bought a new greenhouse, then any warranty will not cover damage due to not having a proper greenhouse base.

Your greenhouse is built on this foundation and base, which will ensure it is easier to erect and that it will last. There are some different choices for the foundation, which we'll talk about now.

Compacted Soil

If you compact the soil enough, then you can build your greenhouse directly on the ground, particularly if you live in an area where the ground doesn't freeze too badly.

A lot of greenhouses will come with an optional metal plinth that has spiked in each corner. These can be cemented into the ground to prevent the base from moving.

You will still need to level the ground, though, so dig out your spirit level. Use a roller or other mechanical device to compact the soil to ensure it is stable. Do not build your base out of gravel or hardcore because these are just not stable enough.

The advantage of using the soil as your foundation is that it is very cost-effective. You can also use the existing ground for growing your plants in, plus drainage is a lot better.

The downside of soil is that it will allow pests into your greenhouse. You will find this particularly bad in winter as pests flock to your greenhouse for the warmth.

Perimeter Bases

This is a slightly cheaper option where you use either bricks, breeze blocks, or thin paving or edging slabs to create a foundation directly under the greenhouse frame. You can use concrete if you prefer.

The foundation is built along where the frame will run, leaving the soil in the middle of the greenhouse untouched.

While you can build the foundation directly on the soil, most people will cut out a trench and place the foundation in the trench. The advantage of this latter approach is that it is easier to level.

Slabs or Paving

This is a very popular way to build your greenhouse foundation because it keeps out the weeds and pests while giving you a good, clean, growing environment.

This method involves building a base the size of your greenhouse out of paving slabs and then fixing your greenhouse to it. This type of base will last for many years and is very low maintenance.

You can screw your greenhouse to the base to provide stability in windy conditions, preventing any damage. It also provides good drainage when compared to an all-concrete base.

In the winter months, a soil floor can get damp and encourage mold to grow. A paved floor helps to keep the greenhouse both warmer and drier in the cooler months.

Providing you bed down the slabs properly with an inch or two of sand underneath them, they are surprisingly easy to get level and will not warp or move over time.

Concrete Base

This is where you mark out where your greenhouse will be and dig down a few inches before pouring concrete in to form the base.

For larger greenhouses, this has its advantages, but it can be expensive and does require special tools such as a concrete mixer.

This is a very durable base, and you can fit expansion bolts to secure larger structures. You may have an issue with standing water, so you may want to consider putting drainage holes in to prevent standing water.

Plastic Resin

These are very attractive and are very popular. This is because, compared to aluminum, they are less expensive, and they also do not conduct any heat away from the greenhouse-like steel does.

Unfortunately, they lack the strength of the metal frames, and can only be used for the smaller greenhouses, with shorter dimensions.

They can only be used with polycarbonate panels.

Wood

Wooden frames are ideal for a simple do-it-yourself greenhouse project. Wood is beautiful and provides sufficient durability and strength, but it is susceptible to rotting; therefore, it doesn't allow contact with moisture.

Tempered Glass

These are strong and impact-resistant.

This means that they will withstand any expansions or contractions during the seasonal temperature changes.

The 3 mm single pane thickness is ideal for the greenhouse.

However, the 4mm thickness is much stronger and will provide additional insulation. You must protect the hedges during insulation, as the glass may shatter if hit hard. Tempered glass is much more expensive compared to polycarbonate panels.

Tempered glass is more durable even if it's expensive, and it is more resistant to scratches, as well as being very clear and providing no diffusion.

Fiberglass

This is translucent and provides a light that is well-diffused. Fiberglass retains heat better than normal glass. The greenhouses made from fiberglass are normally corrugated to provide adequate rigidity because the outer coat will become sunbaked within 6-10 years. The surface will become etched and yellow.

Polycarbonate

It is UV-treated, lightweight and durable. It is high quality and modern material used for greenhouses. The polycarbonate is available in different levels of thickness and provides the clarity of glass, but it's not scratch resistant, or as strong as tempered glass.

The single-walled one does not retain any heat and provides no light diffusion. It, however, has a longer lifespan of more than 15 years, depending on the region.

Twin-Walled Polycarbonate

This is very popular because it has internal spaces providing strength and excellent insulation. The best point to note about the twin-walled polycarbonate is that it diffuses light.

Triple-Walled Polycarbonate

This is similar to twin-walled polycarbonate, but it has extra strength and heat retention abilities. In cold climates, the triple-walled polycarbonate is extremely useful for all-year-round indoor gardening, because it will withstand snow loads and will freeze without cracking or distorting.

Wind Securities

Any surface such as a wall, fence, or even nearby buildings can act as protection against gusts of wind or even snow. When plants are close to these surfaces, they can leech onto the small amount of warmth that they provide. During summer, if your plants cannot stand the heat, you can use these surfaces as sunblock.

CHAPTER 5:

Best Greenhouse Equipment And Accessories

Efficient greenhouse equipment and accessories can be critical to the successful operation of the greenhouse.

To be able to grow high-quality, year-round crops, you would need to know what kind of greenhouse equipment you need to buy. Let's look at the best greenhouse equipment and supplies required when beginning greenhouse gardening:

Best Greenhouse Equipment You Need

One of the main features of an effective greenhouse design is getting the right accessories to make growing crops easier:

1. Basic
2. Greenhouse Furniture
3. Water Management — Irrigation and Drainage
4. Lighting
5. Heating and Climate control
6. Ventilation
7. Pest Control

Each of these components must be prepared for the design of the greenhouses. As you read on, we're going to explore the various things that come in each group.

Basic Greenhouse Equipment

These are the fundamental things that you need to start growing plants.

Container

Your choice of greenhouse containers is essential because it will have a significant influence on how your vegetables or plants grow. Gardeners can use almost anything that grips the soil as long as it meets two criteria for a greenhouse container:

- First, it should promote good health, provide plenty of rooting space and provide excellent drainage.
- Second, it should keep the crop well and stabilize its upward production.

There are different kinds of containers, such as flats and tubes, hanging baskets, and pans.

There are also larger containers that are designed to accommodate a variety of smaller pots.

Hanging baskets are ideal for growing plants, flowers, and vegetables in height while making good use of space. It can be made of plastic, metal-ceramic, or even coconut fiber.

Plugs and flat containers are also used for early germination purposes. These containers are available to accommodate several small plants or flowers while keeping them apart. As far as potting is concerned, gardeners prefer greenhouse pots made of clay because they are the traditional way to grow flowers and plants. However, you can also consider materials such as plastic, wood, peat moss, and wood fiber. They are also lighter in weight, more durable, and cheaper than clay pots. They're also easily disposable.

Seed Boxes

Seed boxes are also considered essential greenhouse equipment. Plastic seed boxes take over from the wooden boxes used by many growers in the past. The pros and cons of plastic against wood are still being explored across the world. If you want to go green, cut off the plastic option and stick with the wood. However, get seed boxes that are around 14 inches X 8 inches X 2 inches. It is the ideal size for rising baby seeds. Rain Chains like these copper rain chains are another perfect product touch.

Furniture to Store Your Greenhouse Equipment and Plants

Well-planned furniture plus adequate shelving inside a greenhouse is essential for the storage of all your pots and containers. In a tight, space-limited greenhouse system, shelving will improve the growing area without negative impacts on the shade.

Shelves may be made from materials such as glass, wood, or metal. It is necessary to note that the amount of lighting entering plants can be affected if double shelving is used. You can also find shelves under garden benches to save space. Greenhouse shelves may be temporary for starting seedlings or permanently attached to the greenhouse structure.

Cinder, wooden blocks, and metal are suitable for legs and tables. The wire mesh of the shelves makes it possible to remove excess water. Greenhouse shelving can also help keep crops apart to avoid seeding or cross-pollination. Garden benches are one type of shelving that allows maximum room and storage.

In general, their ideal size is determined by the width of the hothouse to maximize the through space. Benches can be permanent or temporary fixtures. If you plan to delete or rearrange them regularly, then sectioned bench options can be ideal for you.

Planters are another kind of greenhouse furniture that is commonly used in today's gardening environment. Large and deep seedlings are generally recommended for food crops. They can be made from a range of materials, such as plastic, wood, or metal. They are usually organized in such a way that each planter contains only one vegetable.

Greenhouse Irrigation and Drainage

Systems over their lifetimes, you will need ways to water your plants. Though automatic watering systems are all crazy, there will always be a special place in traditional gardening for good old watering cans. T

he long beams on the cans will comfortably touch all the plants, including at the back of the flower bed.

Greenhouse Water Management

You will likewise be able to customize your watering experience depending on what each bed needs. Plastics also take over metal in the watering can section. Plastic containers are usually smaller, making watering less labor-intensive. Plus, they're also cheaper. But if you have greenhouse aesthetics, stick to the metal cans. The trickle watering system is another form of greenhouse equipment.

Greenhouse Trickle Watering System

Build a plastic hose rinse system with outlet nozzles at various intervals across its duration. Place the hose around your pots in acceptable proximity. Attach your hose to a storage tank that keeps filling and releases water when it's finished. What's great about this system is that you're going to water your pots or beds in the exact quantity you want, at the exact time every day!

Other types of greenhouse water treatment equipment that you may need are good pumps, water breakers, valves, pumps, hoses, sprinklers, and temperature control boilers. Remember, you're going to have to find a place in your greenhouse or yard to store these things.

Greenhouse Lighting

The lighting system inside the greenhouse determines the level of sunlight, artificial light, and shade of the plants. If the sunlight in your area isn't strong enough, you might need to consider artificial lighting.

- Grow lights
- Seedling lights
- Leds
- General all-purpose lighting
- High-intensity lights

Providing a vast lighting network can be costly for small greenhouses, for larger ones, it is almost necessary.

Climate Control and Heating Greenhouse Equipment

These are often a few types of greenhouse equipment designed to control the amount of moisture, heat, and frost inside the greenhouse. Let's look at the main components of the climate control system:

Greenhouse Thermometers

The key to a successful greenhouse is to maintain perfect temperatures at all times, making the thermometer very important. Install a maximum and minimum temperature thermometer with a needle location that appears when the mercury is removed. When it comes to greenhouse thermometers, you're going to need one that can be reset with a magnet.

There are more high-end options with push-button readjustments, but they are not necessary. All types of greenhouses, even portable ones, require thermometers. Often, call a soil thermometer to determine the temperature of the soil.

Greenhouse Thermostat

A greenhouse thermostat helps you to know the current temperature in your greenhouse and to control it accordingly. The temperature gauge or thermometer indicates the temperature changes while the thermostat automatically controls the temperature in the desired area. Ideally, a good greenhouse is expected to have a thermostat.

Greenhouse Heaters

Other critical greenhouse equipment deals with the control of heat inside the greenhouse. Greenhouse heaters are needed to control the temperature of the greenhouse. They come in different types, with different modes and sources of energy. You can choose from electric, gas, and propane heaters according to your needs and requirements. You also have the choice of either choosing a sold or non-vented heater.

Greenhouse Humidistat

Greenhouse humidifiers or humidistats are needed to check the quantity of moisture in the greenhouse. Some plants are sensitive to dry air, which will impede their vegetative growth. With the aid of an appropriate humidistat, this problem can easily be solved.

Ventilation Equipment for Your Greenhouse

Proper ventilation is compulsory for adequate plant growth, not only during certain seasons but throughout the year. This is because, at any time of year, the sun is capable of causing extreme temperature changes. A reasonable rule of thumb is to have open venting options equal to around 20% of the floor space. Vents can be found on the roof and sides of the structure as well as part of the entrance. Roof venting is considered to be the absolute best when it comes to fixing venting systems. Many automated venting systems are the perfect choices for those who are not around to handle the greenhouse all day. Exhaust fans are another way to vent excess air, but whether or not they are a good option for any case, in particular, they deserve analysis.

Pest Control Equipment

No list of greenhouse equipment will be full without pest control equipment. There are several methodologies for effective pest control; some use chemicals, and others use biology. Chemicals are easy to use and relatively cheap, but others may argue that they do more harm than good.

Natural methods, such as the use of what is generally referred to as "beneficial insects," are another type of pest control. Mostly, these bugs track down and eat the bugs that kill your garden. Often all the plant wants is a decent mesh to keep the pests out. These meshes may be made of metal, fabric, or thin plastic. You would also need fencing and door sweeps to keep bugs out of particular areas. Various kinds of fogging machines and sprayers kill bugs. Insecticides and pesticides should be used sparingly, ideally using organic or natural sprays to prevent pests from damaging crops.

Soil Sterilizers

Whatever soil you are considering for planting, it would be extremely helpful to make use of a sterilizer. There are several ways to sterilize the soil, but the easiest and most effective way to do so is by using a steam sterilization system. Steam systems are advantageous and inexpensive. They're not going to take up a lot of space and do a fantastic job on your soil.

Gardening Sieve – Sowing Sieve

The soil texture is an important consideration when planting baby plants. A sowing sieve will be very useful in helping you to achieve the perfect texture. You can use a mesh sieve to cover your seeds with compost after you plant them gently. The good news is that you don't necessarily need to buy a sieve. This piece of greenhouse equipment could be a DIY idea.

Use a small wooden box like those in which you buy bulk produce. Take the bottom of the box and put a piece of perforated zinc in it, and voila — you've got your sieve! You can also assign this essential task to your children and your relatives.

Plant Support Equipment

You will need to provide adequate support to ensure that your plants grow in strength and length. Sometimes, all you have to do is tie the plants together so that they can support each other. Although there are many materials used to bind your plants, we recommend Raphia as it is moderately priced and can help most plants. Many greenhouse growers often use broken loops, green growing twines, and paper-covered wires. Fencing and greenhouse molds can also be used to shape plants into the desired shapes.

CHAPTER 6:

Seed Starting

One of the biggest benefits of a greenhouse is it gives you somewhere to start your seedlings off, so you get a head start on the growing season. Even a small, plastic portable greenhouse out in your garden is sufficient to start your seeds off, and the extra warmth means you can get a really good head start on the year.

Germinating seeds is something many of us will do every year, but it is often touch-and-go as to whether or not they will germinate. It can be hard to find enough space to germinate all the seeds that you want to plant, and you end up not planting some crops you wanted to grow. A greenhouse is a real boon because it gives you plenty of space to start your seeds in a protected environment.

You then need a decent growing medium. A good, peat-based seed compost is a good place to start though you can mix up your own formulas. Avoid cheap compost because it tends to dry out very quickly, have large lumps in and not be as good for your seedlings. You can find your seeds rot before they germinate because the cheap compost doesn't drain well.

Seed trays and containers are good to get, and we often use ones with plastic lids. This way, we can have a greenhouse within a greenhouse.

There are a huge variety of seed trays on the market, depending on what you're growing, use different seed trays. Larger cell trays are used for larger plants, whereas open trays are used for seeds that can be scattered like beetroot, carrot, and so on.

For some seeds, such as sweetcorn, cardboard tubes (such as those found inside toilet rolls) are good to use because the seedlings do not like being handled. The tubes can be planted straight in the ground, and the cardboard will rot as the seedling grows.

Larger plants such as squashes are best sown in individual pots so they can grow to a decent size without having to be re-potted, which they can object to.

You can use peat pots to grow your seedlings in though I have found these have a habit of either drying out too much or becoming sodden and then rotting. Some people like these but I'm not keen on them.

All of these can be sat in seed trays to make it easier for you to organize your plants. Just remember that you have to pick out your seedlings and re-pot them when they get to a certain size and certain types of plants will not appreciate this.

Heat mats can be used to help with germination, but they are not necessary. If you live in a really cold climate, then they are a benefit, but it does require that you have electricity in your greenhouse, which not everyone will have. You also have the expense of buying the heat mats, so you may get one or two to start off your most important or delicate seedlings.

You need to think about the light requirements of each plant because some seedlings prefer more light to others. More sun-sensitive seedlings will need shading from the heat of the midday sun.

One useful technique when sowing seeds in individual pots is to place two or three seeds into each pot, spaced out evenly. This way, if one or two seeds do not germinate, you still have a third which could grow. If all three grow, then you can either prick out and re-plant the three seedlings, or you can discard the smaller seedlings, keeping the strongest.

All seeds need to be covered by the growing medium but not too deeply otherwise, they will not push through the soil to the light. Check the packets to determine exactly how deeply to plant each seed.

For bigger seeds, it is easy to poke them into the soil. One thing to remember with larger seeds, such as squash seeds, is to plant them on their sides so they can grow the right way up. If they are put in the ground the wrong way, then you can find the roots coming up through the soil and the leaves growing underground! This often happens when children help with the planting.

For smaller seeds, you need to cover them with a sprinkling of soil to stop them from blowing away. With smaller seeds, you will need to be careful watering them as they can float away with excess water!

Seeds can take anything from a few days to a few weeks to germinate, depending on the type of plant you are growing. Check the packet for specific timings, so you know when to start checking your seedlings.

During this time, you need to keep them moist, but not wet otherwise, the seeds can rot. Check the pots regularly and make sure they are not too damp. Peat pots can go moldy if the humidity is too high, so you need to keep an eye on them too.

Check the instructions and plant during the time they state. Remember that with a greenhouse, you can start your seedlings earlier in cooler areas than you can outside.

Hardening Off

Not all of your seedlings are going to spend their lives in your greenhouse; some will be planted outside. Moving a plant from the protective enclosure that is your greenhouse into the great outdoors can be an incredible shock to the system. The difference in environments causes shock, which can at best stunt the growth of your plant by several weeks, and at worst, kill it!

Hardening off your seedlings is vital if you want them to survive and thrive when you plant them outside of your greenhouse. You will be surprised how many people don't do this and struggle to get their plants to grow.

The process of hardening off isn't done overnight and can take a week or two, depending on the weather where you live. You will have to be patient, but it is worth it as it strengthens your plants and ensures they grow well.

Once there is no risk of frost during the day, you take your seedlings out of your greenhouse and leave them outside during the day. Put them somewhere that is warm but not too sunny, and that is sheltered from the wind.

Leave your seedlings outside for most of the day, and then mid to late afternoon, move them back into your greenhouse.

Repeat this for 2 or 3 days and then gradually move them into sunnier locations and leave them out for longer.

After a couple of weeks, the seedlings should be in the location where they are to be planted and be left out all day and throughout the night.

Should your plants show any sign of stress such as browning, wilting, or yellowing, then move the hardening process back a step and try again the following day.

Water well during this process, and then after the 2 weeks, you should be able to plant your seedlings out in the ground. It is worth observing them as some may benefit from horticultural fleece or a cloche if the weather starts to get cold or if there is a surprise frost.

Sorting Your Seed Packets

Most gardeners will have seeds packets pretty much everywhere, in drawers, on shelves, tucked away in cupboards. They accumulate, and it is far too easy to get overwhelmed by them. You know what it is like, you get halfway through the growing season and realize you forgot to plant something because you couldn't find the seeds!

There are plenty of different ways for you to organize your seed packets, and it is up to you how best you do it. However, we would strongly recommend that you do organize them because it will make your life easier throughout the growing season and save you money from buying duplicate seed packets.

Firstly, sort the seeds into three piles:

1. Herbs
2. Flowers
3. Vegetables

These are stored separately. Each seed packet is filed under the first month in which it can be planted. Remember that if a seed packet states it can be planted out in a month, then you can often start the seedling off in a greenhouse between 4 and 8 weeks earlier, depending on whether it is heated or not!

A greenhouse is a real boon when it comes to starting off seedlings and will help you get a head start on the growing season. It also gets the seed trays out of the house and gives your plants a great start in life. Many growers tend to ask the difference between vegetables, herbs, and fruits. A vegetable is a plant or any part of a plant that is considered edible and can be eaten. Herbs, on the other hand, refer to plants or parts of plants that are grown as food and also for medicinal purposes while fruits are eatable products containing seeds that are formed from the matured ovary of a flowering plant. The major difference is that while fruits can be referred to as vegetables, vegetables cannot exactly be termed fruits. Also, it is arguable that not all herbs are eaten as the main ingredient, as is the case of vegetables.

CHAPTER 7:

How To Grow A Garden In Greenhouse

You owe your plants the best conditions to develop and flourish, so readiness is significant. It is feasible to set up the dirt for spring's development during fall or develop a couple of winter crops in case you're available. In the event that you give your best to satisfactory planning and setting up, your nursery will move your neighbors to have their garden the accompanying season.

Sun

Be careful with shadows when you are situating your plants. Shadows diminish the measure of daylight that a plant will get, prompting hindered development, bugs rearing, and illnesses. Most of the nursery vegetables require 7 hours of daylight each day to yield their best.

In the light of this prerequisite, you should stay away from shadows from trees, encompassing structures, or whatever other tall construction that can obstruct daylight from arriving at the plants.

When settling on your nursery's area throughout the colder time of year, remember that deciduous trees shed their leaves during winter and develop them again throughout the spring.

Positioning

Situating ought to be given satisfactory thought since it is one of the factors that impact how much your plant will blossom and the measure of gather you will get from a specific harvest. You can set your bed on your patio as long as you are certain of the lighting in case you are managing little space issues. A raised bed delivers more gather from a restricted space on the grounds that more yields can be planted, and they can be put more like each other when the in-line strategy is embraced.

Drainage

The raised situation of the raised bed will further develop seepage; still, you shouldn't be casual about offering thought to the plants' seepage necessity. Raised bed gardens don't do well in damp or low-lying regions on the grounds that these regions are effortlessly overwhelmed.

The Breadth of The Bed

Raised bed garden appreciates free soil on the grounds that nobody strolls or steps on it like in a customary nursery. The bed size assumes a critical part in whether your soil will get stepped on or not. Suggested estimations for a raised bed are 4 x 4 feet for youngsters and teens, and 6 x 6 feet for adults.

Stretch similar to you easily can, the catchphrase here being serenely, and name where you can reach with your hand with a marker; this should give you a harsh thought of the bed estimation that you can advantageously work with. You ought to 2-fold to measure from the point you bowed to the detect that you came to have your garden square's length. On the off chance that you can easily arrive at three feet, you ought to have a bed of 6 x 6 feet.

Aeration

Phenomenal air conveyance is required for a healthy nursery. Air circulation assists with some fundamental things, like vigorous stem development, the anticipation of bugs, molds, and in general, plant wellbeing. Since you need your plants to be sufficiently circulated air through, you ought to be mindful so as not to open them to overabundance wind. At the equivalent time, anything that will obstruct the consistent flow of air, similar to a nursery straightforwardly close to a fence, ought to be kept away from. To have the perfect measure of air in your nursery, your plants will move to and for tenderly in the breeze.

Water

As said before, soil in a raised bed warms up quicker; subsequently, they dry out comparably much. Hence, your nursery ought to be found near a water source. We don't figure anybody can stand to continue to go to their nursery a few times every day essentially to water; there is a day-to-day existence outside the nursery. There are a few ways to deal with watering; the expensive yet simple strategy that accomplished landscapers like, which is water lines and ice-free hydrant in the nursery. There is additionally a modest strategy for fledglings, which is to run a hose into the nurseries.

Designs

You can make your nursery any state of your decision; that is one of the manufacturers' advantages. Nobody said it should be a square. Most of the plants are planted in 2 columns, with an individual line around one foot along the length, however, some like garlic, onions, and corns are planted in succession. We love to develop in an enormous region of land, however not fitting for an amateur; it is incredible in light of the fact that it delivers new vegetables for a family and extra for neighbors and visitors.

Planning

The nursery's size ought to be the following thing at the forefront of your thoughts in the wake of choosing its position and arrangement. Try not to be feeling the squeeze to have a major nursery; a bed as little as 4 x 4 feet is OK. This measurement will yield a greater number of harvests than its conventional partner of a similar estimation. Likewise, the sort of plant you need to develop will impact, somewhat, the size of your nursery. Planting tomatoes in a four x four-foot bed will imply that each corner will have one tomato plant.

First-time nursery workers should begin with a couple of their harvests after they have affirmed that proposals wanted yields will flourish in their environment. It is better regardless only one bed since its support will not be excessively depleting or unpleasant in the main year. Over the long haul, add additional beds on the off chance that you have space and assets.

Depth

Various plants call for various profundities, so you need to settle on your profundity in view of what you need to develop around the season. Minimal profundity for a raised bed, independent of what you plan to develop, is seven inches, however, it tends to be higher. Root crops like parsnips or carrots 10 – 15 inches profundity to develop uninhibitedly.

CHAPTER 8:

Growing Vegetables, Herbs, And Fruits

Any growers tend to ask the difference between vegetables, herbs, and fruits. A vegetable is a plant or any part of a plant that is considered edible and can be eaten. Herbs, on the other hand, refer to plants or part of plants that are grown as food and also for medicinal purposes while fruits are eatable products containing seeds which are formed from the matured ovary of a flowering plant. The major difference is that while fruits can be referred to as vegetables, vegetables cannot exactly be termed fruits. Also, it is arguable that not all herbs are eaten as the main ingredient, as is the case of vegetables.

Herbs

Herb gardens are hip and happening these days. Neighbors, companions, family... Everyone has one. Regardless of whether you have a huge or a little nursery, there is constantly a spot where you can develop a few herbs. Be that as it may, how to begin? Beneath, you will discover 7 tips that will assist you with beginning with your herb garden.

1. **Pick your preferred herbs:** Before you start making your own herb garden, you ought to pick which herbs to develop. Pick the herbs that you like utilizing best. Consider which suppers you set up the most, and which fixings your requirement for those. Or on the other hand, consider mixes of herbs that you can use in a summery mixed drink. For example, rosemary is tasty in a reviving Gin and Tonic. Be that as it may, hello, you didn't hear it from me. On the off chance that you grow a variety of herbs immediately, it may become work seriously. That is on the grounds that all herbs require a particular consideration routine, and before you realize it, you're going through hours on them. So, make a determination and spotlight on those. Achievement is ensured!

2. **Keep your herbs inside from the start:** In case you need to plant the herbs yourself, it's ideal to begin inside. Along these lines, the seeds will develop a lot quicker. Sow them in little window boxes and ensure that overabundance of water can deplete. At the point when it quits freezing around evening time, you can steadily begin putting the plants outside. Put them out a little longer each time with the goal that they can become acclimated to the temperatures.

3. **Try not to stand by too long to even think about transferring your herbs to a vegetable nursery box:** On the off chance that you begin developing your herbs inside, don't stand by too long to even consider

transferring them outside. In the event that you do, they will transform into long floppy stalks, attempting to develop towards the light. When the climate licenses, you ought to report them to a grower or vegetable nursery box. Talking about which, those are additionally perfect for an overhang or porch. That way, you generally include your herbs within reach. If there's a chance that the climate is awful, you can simply put them inside. One thing you should focus on while picking a vegetable nursery box is that you pick one that is made of maintainable materials that are impervious to wind and climate. It is ideal for picking one made of aluminum, a tropic wood type, or weatherproof pine. That will guarantee that you can appreciate it for a considerable length of time without an excessive amount of upkeep. Progressively about picking the correct sort of wood.

4. **Consolidate the correct herbs:** Not all herbs require a similar consideration, which is the reason it is ideal for joining herbs with a similar consideration routine in a similar grower or herb bed. Mediterranean herbs, for example, rosemary, thyme, lavender, oregano, and sage, appreciate full sun and not all that much water. Basil, chives, and parsley, then again, favor drinking somewhat more.

5. **Save your herbs for the winter:** Do you like cooking with herbs from your own nursery all through the winter? At that point, make little packages of the herbs and hang them topsy-turvy in a dry and warm region. At the point when they have dried, you can store them in a cool and dim spot, in a holder or resealable sack. Do you lean toward freezing your herbs? At that point, save them in the cooler for a limit of a half year.

Vegetables

1. On the off chance that it's getting cold and you have tomatoes, despite everything maturing on the vine—spare your tomatoes! Pull the plants up, then bring them inside to a warm, dry spot. Hang them up, and the tomatoes will mature on the vine.
2. Friend planting is a superb method to improve your nursery. A few plants renew supplements lost by another, and a few mixes successfully ward bugs off.
3. Paint the handles of your nursery instrument a brilliant, shading other than green to assist you with discovering them among your plants. You can likewise save a letter drop in your nursery for simple instrument stockpiling.
4. The fertilizer needs time to coordinate and balance out in the dirt. Apply a little while before planting.
5. To blend fertilizer into your dirt without a great deal of overwhelming work, spread the manure over your nursery in the pre-winter after all the reaping is finished. Spread with a winter mulch, for example, roughage or cleaved leaves, and let nature follow through to its logical end. By spring, the softening day off soil, living beings will have worked the manure in for you.
6. Like vining vegetables; however, you haven't got the room? Train your melons, squash, also cucumbers onto a vertical trellis or fence. Spares space and looks pretty as well.
7. Nursery vegetables that become over-ready are an obvious objective for certain irritations. Expel them as quickly as time permits, maintaining a strategic distance from recognition.
8. Onions are prepared to collect when the tops have fallen over. Let the

dirt dry out, collect, and store in a warm, dry, dull spot until the tops dry. Remove the foliage down to an inch, store it in a cool, dry territory.

9. Keep earth off lettuce also the cabbage leaves when developing by spreading a 1–2-inch layer of mulch around each plant. This additionally helps hold the weeds down.

10. When you are planting a blossom or vegetable transplant, store a bunch of manure into each opening. The fertilizer will give transplants and additional lift that endures all through the developing season.

11. Bugs can't stand plants, for example, garlic, onions, chives, and chrysanthemums. Develop these plants around the nursery to help repulse creepy crawlies.

12. For simple peas, start them inside. The germination rate is far superior, and the seedlings will be more advantageous and better ready to ward off nuisances and aliments.

13. Sound soil implies solid plants that are better ready to oppose nuisances and infection, diminishing the requirement for hurtful pesticides.

Fruits

Such huge numbers of various types of fruit are accessible, so how would you start to conclude which to develop? Start with quality. At the point when delicate berries are homegrown, they can be gathered when completely ready, stout, and sweet, without worry for transportation and perishability. The flavor is remarkable.

The measure of nursery space accessibility will be another integral factor. Pick between developing little fruits (berries that develop on little plants, vines, or hedges) or bigger tree fruits. Start with effortlessly raised, space-productive little fruits, for example, strawberries, blackberries, and raspberries. In any case, you have a spot in your scene for a fruit tree or two, don't leave behind the chance. Search for simple consideration fruit trees or even nontraditional trees, for example, mulberries or crabapples.

Fruits that Grow on Trees

Conventional plantation trees, for example, apples, peaches, pears, and fruits, require some information and thoughtfulness regarding fertilization, pruning, bother control, treating, and different sorts of care. To limit or wipe out disease splash, search for new, disease-safe apple cultivars.

Plant overshadows fruit trees, which remain little enough for you to pick the fruit starting from the earliest stage. This is a sheltered, simple approach to collect. You won't need to carry around stepping stools or parity on them while working. Another preferred position of smaller person fruit trees is they start to tolerate fruit a lot more youthful than full-size trees do. What's more, if your garden is little, a diminutive person tree, which occupies less room than its full-size partner, is a decent other option.

Have a go at growing a super-predominate peach tree in a pot. Super-midgets are extra-smaller than normal trees that may arrive at just around 5 feet tall. Albeit other fruit trees come as super-smaller people, peaches produce tasty fruit with just one tree and are extraordinary for apprentices. (Numerous other fruit trees require a second cultivar for fertilization).

Plant your super-predominate peach tree in a 24-inch-wide tub with waste gaps in the base. Keep it damp, very much treated, and in a radiant area during the developing season. On the off chance that your tree doesn't prove to be fruitful the principal year, give it time. It might require one more year or two to begin its vocation. During winter, in chilly atmospheres, store the tree, tub and all, in a cool but ensured area.

Utilize clingy red balls that look like apples for control of slimy apple parasites on apple and plum trees. Apple parasites are fly hatchlings that burrow into creating fruit, making it nauseating and unappetizing.

Apple parasite flies are effortlessly tricked, notwithstanding. In the event that you put out clingy red balls that take after apples (natively constructed or bought through a nursery supply index), the egg-laying females will be pulled into the ball and stall out. (This will end their egg-laying vocation!) Hang at any rate one clingy red ball in a smaller person tree and at least six in bigger trees.

Use tree groups to find slithering irritations in ascending fruit tree trunks. Clingy plastic groups will find ants conveying aphids and crawling caterpillars, for example, vagabond moths and codling moths.

CHAPTER 9:

Health Benefits Of Growing In Your Greenhouse

Improves Your Well-Being

Ost of us know we are supposed to consume more fruits and vegetables daily. It is not just great advice from the mother. Many vegetables are packed with vitamins A and C, fiber, water, and minerals like potassium. An increasing body of research demonstrates that eating fresh fruits and veggies not only provides your body with vitamins and nutrients needed to operate correctly but also, it shows that lots of fruits and veggies are packed with phytochemicals and antioxidants, certain substances that help fight and prevent disease.

While certain fruits and vegetables are high in certain nutrients, the best method to ensure to receive a fantastic variety of these chemicals on your diet would be to "consume a rainbow" By eating an assortment of different-colored veggies and fruits; you receive all the nutrients that you will need to be healthful.

Can Help You Save Some Money

You will have some savings by growing your fruits and vegetables. In reality, based on the kind and amount you develop, it is possible to save tens of thousands of dollars. By spending several bucks on plants, seeds, and provides in spring, you are going to create veggies that produce pounds of produce in summer. Rather than needing to visit the supermarket to purchase all that create, you have made it ready for the choice for free from your lawn. It is your produce section! You will save hundreds of dollars on your grocery bill every year by developing a garden.

Help The Environment

Your tomatoes, lettuces, and melons in the supermarket store are worth more than just the cost to make them. It is projected that the typical produce travels around 1,500 kilometers to get from farm to supermarket, and that is only fruits and vegetables produced in the USA. Increasingly, produce has been imported from overseas countries, for example, China and Chile. The fossil fuels used to transfer these vegetables grow air pollution and global warming. So, among those big-picture causes of developing your product is to combat these effects on earth. Additionally, by increasing your vegetables, fruits, and veggies, you also lower the total amount of pollution that is made on the farm. Despite it being a traditional or organic farm, lots of big surgeries tend to use a lot of fertilizers, pesticides, and herbicides to cultivate their crops. Regrettably, a number of those additives wind up as resources (and their production requires fossil fuels). By developing your product working with a minimum amount of those inputs, you can cut back on the total amount of fertilizer and chemical contamination that ends up in waterways across the nation.

Raise Your Quality in Life

A less tangible (but significant) reason to cultivate your vegetables is linked to wellbeing. Vegetable gardening is a superb way to unwind after a tough day. You can attain a very simple pleasure and pride in drifting throughout your garden, snacking to a bean and a cherry tomato there, pulling out a few weeds, watering, and enjoying the fruits of your labors. It is a quick, easy gratification in a world that often is complex and complicated. Furthermore, if you garden with other people in a neighborhood garden, you are going to create new friendships and bonds with your neighbors. According to the NGA food gardening poll, over a million neighborhood gardens exist across the nation. Frequently community gardens become a focus for local beautification, education, and improvement projects. If the gardens are sown, folks begin taking interest and pride in their area and the way it seems. Often graffiti, crime, and vandalism are reduced only by producing a garden where people can gather together. And you thought all you're doing is developing a few vegetables.

There are many health benefits of gardening, part of the allure is to make an ordered appearance to the garden. Section of those benefits is producing perfect conditions for crops so that they may be intensively managed to produce top yields in rather tiny places. Greenhouse also gives the capability to cultivate flowers or food in regions that could otherwise be unsuitable.

CHAPTER 10:

Greenhouse Hacks

He purpose and intention of the structure should be to optimize crop growth in the most efficient way possible if you own and operate a greenhouse. While it is true that numerous owners make efforts to achieve designs best suited to their needs and materials for the design they have chosen, these areas of focus will not always lead to the least energy use growth structure. All greenhouse units, regardless of their design and materials, typically serve their unique purpose in creating an optimum growth environment for different crop types.

The true purpose and goal of a greenhouse, however, should not be overlooked, and this is to create an optimal environment for your growing crops that not only reduces time but also greatly saves money.

In this guide, 15 hacks are offered to help you achieve a high degree of efficiency and energy reduction for your greenhouse.

1. Build Conservation. Checklist Conservation is an essential component of basic operation at the cost of high energy use of today's greenhouses. Research suggests that the energy consumed by greenhouses is: 75% of total energy in relation to heating and/or cooling, 15% of the total energy in connection with the supply of electricity to the unit, 10% of the total energy in respect of resources needed for service and servicing.

2. Based on these figures, it is only sensible, to begin with, a conservation checklist that emphasizes energy consumers who could save the most.

This means you should focus on ways to increase efficiency in climate control and electricity use. The first step towards making your greenhouse more efficient is knowing what to focus on and where to start.

3. Assess the structure. The second step in the development of an efficient greenhouse is the assessment of the structure as a whole. This is particularly important if you concentrate on climate control. Cool air or warm air can easily escape from the greenhouse. When trying to keep a certain temperature in the greenhouse, you should understand that your losses will depend on the structure cover and the age of the unit. If you want to heat the structure effectively, consider a double polyethylene cover–which can reduce your heating costs by 50%. When using a glass greenhouse, consider upgrading the structure with a double polyethylene layer–which could reduce costs up to 60%.

4. Eliminate air leaks. It is imperative that you work to prevent any air leaks associated with the structure to ensure that your greenhouse is operating efficiently. The main place to begin is the structure door or doors. A special door closing unit should be used, or even a door spring mounted to make sure the air does not enter the unit. Weatherstripping should also be placed around the unit openings, like doors, windows, and ventilation units. The strip should also be placed around openings close to fans. If you find holes in the greenhouse siding or Foundation, they should be repaired immediately.

5. If you want to increase the efficiency of your greenhouse, you should focus on doubling the structure coverage. One way to do this is to bubble-wrap the interior walls of the structure. It offers what is called a "thermopane effect" in the device that improves Insulation in the house. If you have an older frame, just throw a double plastic sheet over the

device to reduce the infiltration and minimize heat loss by up to 50%.

6. Implement a conserving curtain. If you want an efficient greenhouse, consider a thermal curtain. Such goods will save from 20 to 50% everywhere. If the cost of the curtain is around $2.50 on average for each square foot, the payback is paid in 2 years. If it costs less, you will be paid sooner.

7. Install Insulation at the Foundation. You should take the time to insulate your Foundation to reduce the efficiency of your greenhouse—the best way to use a board made of polyurethane or polystyrene. The board should be 1 to 2 inches thick and should be placed under the ground approximately 8 inches to help reduce heat loss. In this way, the soil located in the region close to the sides of the structure in the winter months will increase to a total of 10.

8. When you are interested in increasing the amount of heat stored in your greenhouse, the area behind your heating pipes should be isolated. Nevertheless, it is better to use aluminum-faced building paper to help radiate heat from the pipes back onto the growing area of your greenhouse.

9. Consider the location of your structure.

10. To reduce your greenhouse energy consumption, but the structure in an area is surrounded by trees and/or other types of structures. The wind that the unit undergoes over time is a result of a lot of heat loss with growth structures. If you choose to put the building in a sheltered area, it is important to make sure the building always receives the correct light so that the crops continue to grow properly.

11. The next step in optimizing greenhouse energy efficiency is to place windbreaks on the north side of the edifice as well as on the northwest side. In these areas, you might put several coniferous trees or even a

plastic snow fence. This reduces the amount of heat loss by wind exposure.

12. Increase the amount of space in your Greenhouse One of the most productive ways to maximize greenhouse efficiency is to increase your unit space. You can improve the amount of space you have up to 90% with benches that can be moved or peninsular shaped. You should mount racks that can be stacked if you have small plants. Furthermore, in baskets that can be placed on rails or on overhead transport systems, you can grow crops.

13. Regular heating system maintenance if you want to save time and money by optimizing the greenhouse efficiency, make sure your heating system maintains regularly. You should make sure the boiler works optimally and is periodically cleaned. You should have a furnace regularly changed and washed. If you have a medium unit, this may save hundreds of gallons of petroleum per year.

14. Use Electronic Thermostats you should convert to an electronic model if you currently use an electronic thermostat. In so doing, you will find that up to 500 gallons of heating fuel can be saved each year. The implementation of these thermostats will also lead to more precise temperature measurements. Mechanical units have been measured to read sometimes up to two degrees higher than electronic devices. This could result in expenses exceeding $200.00 per year. You can avoid paying too much to control your structure's climate by switching to an electronic thermostat.

15. Install fans; the next way to maximize the output of the greenhouse is to install fans generating horizontal airflow.

16. Try using open-roof cooling strategies. When you spend a lot of money cooling your greenhouse, you can try open-roof designs. This

form of design removes the need for fans and high-priced refrigeration systems.

17. Finally, if you want to optimize your greenhouse efficiency, you should install energy lighting systems. The use of moving bulbs and lights is known to be an efficient device that saves you hundreds of dollars per year.

CHAPTER 11:

Greenhouse Irrigation Systems

One of the main issues you will face with a greenhouse is keeping your plants watered. In hot weather, they can dry out very quickly, and this can cause problems such as leaf, flower or fruit drop, which you obviously want to avoid.

If your greenhouse is in your garden, then it is easy enough to pop down and water it, but if it is at an allotment or you are on holiday, then watering becomes much trickier, putting your harvest at risk.

In the hottest weather, and more so in hotter climates, you will need to water your plants 2 or 3 times a day to keep them healthy no matter how good your cooling system is!

Although you can hand-water the plants in your greenhouse, this can soon get boring and difficult to keep up with. The best and most efficient way to water your plants is to invest in a greenhouse irrigation system. Which you choose will depend on the size of your greenhouse, what you are growing and whether or not you have electricity and water to hand.

If you are planning to irrigate your greenhouse, then the need to be sited near to water and/or electricity can heavily influence your choice of location.

There are plants that require more water than others, so depending on what you are growing, you may want to get an automatic irrigation system that can deliver differing quantities of water to different plants.

You also want a system that can grow with you as you put more plants in your greenhouse. At certain times within the season, you will have more plants in your greenhouse than at others, so your irrigation system needs to be able to support this extra demand.

You do need to be careful because any irrigation system that is introducing too much water to your greenhouse could end up making it too damp, which will encourage the growth of diseases. This is one reason why you need to have your drainage and ventilation right to prevent damage to your greenhouse ecosystem.

You typically have 2 choices about how to deliver water to your plants, either through spray heads or a drip system. The former will spray water over everything in your greenhouse. The downside of it is that it can encourage powdery mildew on certain plants, but the spray can help damp down your greenhouse. It can also be a bit hit and miss as to how much ends up in the soil of your plants. If you are growing in containers, then a spray system may not deliver water precisely enough.

Drip systems though will deliver water precisely to containers and give each container exactly the right amount of water, so no plant goes thirsty! The downside of most irrigation systems is that they require electricity, which can be difficult, expensive, or even impossible for some greenhouse owners to install. You can purchase solar-powered irrigation systems which will do the job, but they can struggle on duller days. The water will come into the greenhouse with piping, and correctly locating this is important. Hanging it from the ceiling and running it along the walls helps keep it out of the way and stops it from getting damaged. Running the piping along the floor is a recipe for disaster as you are bound to end up putting a container on it and damaging it!

You will need a water supply and ideally mains water, but you can run some irrigation systems from water butts. You will have to check regularly that the water butt has enough water in it, but it is still much easier than manually watering your plants!

Overhead Misters

If you grow mostly or all one type of plant, then an overhead watering method is a great choice because you can water all your plants evenly and easily. For larger greenhouses, this is a great system because it will water a large area quickly.

Its downside is that it is quite wasteful of water because the water goes everywhere in the greenhouse, not just into the containers where your plants are. Your plants end up getting a lot of water on their leaves. If they are overcrowded or ventilation is poor, then this can cause problems such as powdery mildew and make your plants more susceptible to disease.

Mat Irrigation

You can buy capillary matting, which works as an irrigation system for your plants. This is a special mat that is designed to draw up water which is then absorbed by your plants through moisture wicks that go into the soil of your containers.

The mat is kept moist by a drip watering system, so you do not have to run water piping throughout your greenhouse. It can just go to strategic points where it feeds the capillary matting.

This is a relatively cheap method of irrigation and is very simple to install. The big advantage is it is very efficient in its use of water, and there is little risk of overwatering your plants!

Drip Tubing

This is special tubing that you run throughout your greenhouse. It has tubes attached to it that run to the roots of each container to supply water directly to the soil. The big advantage of most drip systems is that you can control the amount of water dripping into your plants. This means that plants that need more water can get it, and plants that need less don't get over-watered.

This is set to drip at a certain rate or to operate on a timer so it waters at regular intervals. It will depend on the type of system you buy as to whether it is constant or timed. Timed is by far the best as it allows greater control of the delivery of water, reducing the risks of over-watering.

This is a very water-efficient method of watering your greenhouse with minimal wastage. It can also be set up to be completely automatic, which reduces the time you spend managing your greenhouse.

With some of the more advanced drip watering systems, you have sensors in the ground that monitor moisture levels and turn on the water when the soil becomes too dry.

If you are growing directly in the soil, then the type of soil will influence your drip-rate. A heavy clay soil will take longer to absorb water, so it needs less water than a lighter soil because in clay, it will puddle and pool, which you want to avoid.

When you are growing a variety of plants, this is by far the best irrigation method because you can control the water each container receives.

Planning your drip watering system is relatively easy. You need to divide your greenhouse into an equal number of sections, and each area will hold plants with similar water requirements. Depending on the size of the greenhouse, you may need multiple irrigation systems, but most are easy to expand with additional piping.

Drip irrigation piping comes in either black polyethylene (PE) or polyvinyl chloride (PVC). These are cheap, easy to handle, and bendy when you need them to be.

PVC pipe is often used in supply and header lines as you can solvently bond connections and fittings. Polyethylene connections, though need to be clamped. PVC pipe is also more durable, being less sensitive to temperature fluctuations and sunlight, but it is more expensive to buy.

Polyethylene pipe is sensitive to high temperatures and will contract and expand. This means it can move out of position unless it is held in place.

Your main feeder piping may be 1-inch or 2-inch wide, but for lateral, emitter lines, ½-inch piping is sufficient. Each row of plants will have its own ½-inch line containing emitters. In smaller greenhouses, you can get away with one emitter line for every two rows when plants are spaced less than 18-20-inch apart.

There are some different types of emitters available. The perforated hose or porous pipe types are very common and are an emitter lines with holes in it. The water then seeps out of these holes. Most will deliver water at a rate of anywhere from ½ to 3 gallons an hour. The rate of delivery is changed by adjusting the water pressure.

Alternatively, you can get emitter valves which allow you to control the drip rate for each pot. Emitters are usually spaced between 24-inch and 36-inch along the main lateral lines.

One thing to remember is that you need to filter the water, particularly if it is coming out of a water butt. It will prevent any dirt from getting into the system and clogging the emitters. This is vital as it will ensure your irrigation system works without any problems.

Some irrigation systems will allow you to install a fertilizer injector. This is useful as you can get your irrigation system to automatically feed your plants too! Depending on the system, this can be set to deliver liquid fertilizer constantly or at specified intervals. This, though, is typically found in more expensive systems, and you need to be very careful in your choice of liquid feed to prevent clogging up the system.

The key with drip irrigation systems is to apply a little water frequently to maintain the soil moisture levels. This is a very water-efficient system that is easy to expand and works no matter what size plants you are growing.

Most people who own a greenhouse and install an irrigation system will choose a drip watering system. They are easily available and very affordable though, as, with anything, you can spend more money and get more advanced systems.

CHAPTER 12:

Temperature And Humidity For A Greenhouse

Air flow is very important for healthy plant growth in a greenhouse, particularly in the heat of summer as temperatures (hopefully) soar. The air needs to keep moving, which will prevent heat from building up and damaging your plants.

Most greenhouses will come with vents and/or windows to help with the movement of air. A good quality greenhouse will have louver vents at ground level, which draw in cold air (which is heavier than hot air), and then vents at the top that allows hot air to rise out of the greenhouse. This creates a very natural movement of air which your plants appreciate.

You are looking for a greenhouse with windows and vents that account for around a third of the entire roof area. They do not all need to be at roof level, and, ideally, you will want vents at different levels.

If your greenhouse isn't suitably ventilated, then you are going to encourage all sorts of diseases such as fungal problems, powdery mildew, and botrytis. Worse still, a greenhouse that is too hot will end up killing some of your plants.

You can leave the door open in the summer, but this can be a security problem depending on where your greenhouse is located.

The other disadvantage of leaving a door open is that pets, particularly cats, will decide to investigate your greenhouse. Dogs, cats, and chickens will cause havoc in your greenhouse, from eating plants and fruits to sitting on plants. If you do have pets and want to leave the door open, then a wire panel will keep out most animals except cats.

Window or door screens can be used to keep out unwanted visitors, but the downside of these is that they can also keep out vital pollinating insects!

Mice and other rodents can find their way into your greenhouse through open windows or doors, so it can be worth installing an ultrasonic device to keep them out. Of course, cats are excellent rodent deterrents, but they cause their unique brand of chaos!

Shade Cloth and Paint

This is one of the simplest ways for you to provide shade for your plants. Shade paint is applied to the outside of your glass, and it diffuses the sun and keeps some of the heat out. Modern shade paints are very clever and will react to the sunlight. When it is raining, then the shade paint remains clear, but as the sun comes out, the paint turns white, reflects the sunlight.

Shade fabric is another way to cool your greenhouse, and this is put on the outside of your greenhouse to prevent the sunlight from getting to your plants. It is best installed on the outside of your greenhouse, but you can put it inside, though it will not be as effective. When it is outside, it stops the sun's rays from penetrating your greenhouse, but when on the inside, the sunlight is already in the greenhouse and generating heat.

Shading alone though is not going to protect your plants from heat damage. Combine this with good ventilation and humidity control to provide your plants with the best possible growing environment.

Shade cloth is a lightweight polyethylene knitted fabric available in densities from 30% to 90% to keep out less or more of the sun's rays. It is not only suitable for greenhouses but is used in cold frames and other applications. It is mildew and rot resistant, water permeable, and does not become brittle over time.

It provides great ventilation and diffuses the light, keeping your greenhouse cooler. It can help reduce the need to run fans in the summer and is quick to install and remove.

A reflective shade is good because instead of absorbing the sun's rays, it reflects them. This is better if you can get hold of it because it will be more efficient at keeping the greenhouse cool. The reflective shade cloth is more expensive than a normal shade cloth, but it is worth the money for the additional benefits.

For most applications, you will want a shade cloth that is 50–60% density, but in hotter climates or with light-sensitive plants, higher densities such as 70–80% will be necessary. A lot of people use higher-density shade cloth on the roof and lower-density cloth on the walls.

Shade cloth is typically sold by the foot or meter, depending on where you are located, though you can find it sold in pre-made sizes. These are usually hemmed and include grommets for attaching the cloth to the greenhouse.

Shade cloth with a density of 70% allows 30% of light to pass through it. For most vegetables, in the majority of climates, a shade cloth of 30–50% will be sufficient. If you are shading people, then you will want to go up to a density of 80–90%.

Air Flow

Keeping the air moving in your greenhouse during summer can be difficult, particularly in larger greenhouses. Many of the larger electrical greenhouse heaters will double up as air blowers in the summer just by using the fan without the heating element is turned on.

However, using a fan is down to whether or not you have electricity in your greenhouse, which not all of us will have. Although you can use solar energy to run your fan, you will find that it is hard to generate enough energy to keep it going all day.

Choosing an Exhaust Fan

For larger greenhouses, you will want an exhaust fan. This is overkill for a smaller greenhouse, but anyone choosing a larger structure will benefit from installing one.

Your exhaust fan needs to be able to change the air in your greenhouse in between 60 and 90 seconds. Fans are rated by cubic feet per minute (CFM), for which you will need to calculate the volume of your greenhouse, which is done simply by multiplying the length by the width by the average height.

To measure the average height, measure straight down to the floor from halfway up a roof rafter. It doesn't have to be precise, as a few inches either way isn't going to make a significant difference.

To determine the cubic feet per minute rating, you need you simply multiply the volume by ¾. Then you will need to find a fan that is near to or greater than this value.

Be careful and double-check your calculations as a fan that is too small will not provide you with enough cooling. Together with a fan, shading cloth or paint, and damping down, it will help ensure the greenhouse is kept cool and your plants thrive.

As an example, if your greenhouse is 8-inch x 10-inch with an average height of 7-inch, this will give you a calculation of 8x10x7 which is 560 cubic feet.

So, therefore, you will need a fan that is rated at least 560 CFM for sufficient cooling.

You will also need to calculate the shutter size. Do this by dividing your fan Cubic Feet per Minute by 250, which gives a shutter size in ft2.

The fan needs to be positioned as high as possible, typically at the end opposite the door. The motor needs to be on the inside of the greenhouse, and the fan can be mounted either on the inside or outside as convenient for you.

The shutters are installed at the opposite end to the exhaust fan. For those without a motor, they are installed with the vanes opening into your greenhouse. Motorized shutters are installed with the motor on the inside of the greenhouse and the vanes opening outwards.

Ventilating your greenhouse is extremely important and something many growers overlook. Plants need airflow to stay healthy. Poor airflow is a major contributing factor to fungal infections, which plants such as cucumber and tomatoes are particularly susceptible to.

Ensuring your plants are not too crowded will also help a lot with airflow and preventing fungal infections.

Although your greenhouse may be too small for a fan or you may not have any electricity, at the very least, you need windows though louver vents will help a lot. Making sure there is adequate ventilation in your greenhouse is vital, so don't skip this step when setting up your greenhouse!

CHAPTER 13:

Combat Disease And Pest

Remove Bugs and Pests

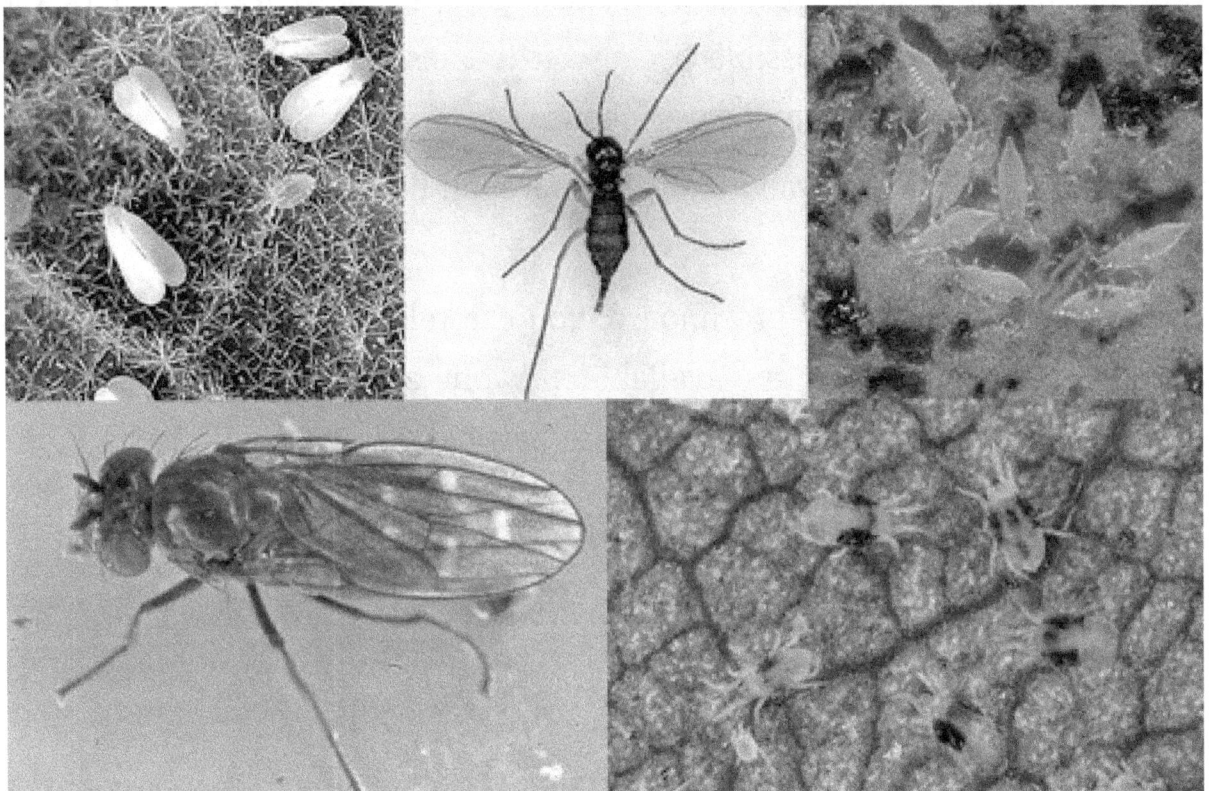

Ash all the benches in the garden with soapy water. Washing the benches and any other table in the greenhouse will enable you to remove dirt and moisture that can cause mold. Always ensure you keep the greenhouse's surface dry, and you can use cloth or a sponge to wipe clean any moisture or damp areas on the surface. Spray any built-up mildew on the walls with mildew spray. You should also clean the area between the panes to avoid a buildup of condensation, leading to the growth of molds and algae.

Clean the flooring area of your structure thoroughly. Some floors are made of wood, gravel, cement, or fabric carpeting, and depending on your greenhouse's floor type, molds can grow. You need to scrub the floor and clean out any mold, mud, and other decaying matter.

Remove any dead plant branches and leaves. Pests or bugs can infect plants, causing the leaves to wither, and prune any dead leaves or branches to prevent further disease spread. You must take the dead leaves out of the greenhouse as soon as possible because if left inside, they may decompose and allow pests or bugs into the greenhouse.

Weeds and any other unimportant plants around the greenhouse area should be removed.

If some pests invade your greenhouse, you can release spiders and ladybugs into the garden, if they are available in your area. If ladybugs are not available in your pet stores, you can use pesticides to deal with pests in the greenhouse instead.

Provide Shade and More Sun

Most greenhouse roofs and windows are made of plastic material or fiberglass. These materials can turn a darker shade caused by overheating from the sun or microscopic molds after some time. This change can reduce the amount of light in the greenhouse.

You should periodically clean the windows to allow light and sun to enter the greenhouse. Consider replacing the roof material after a while. Plant trees that can provide shade for your greenhouse during the summer months, which can act as shade to protect your plants from hot weather. You should plant the trees on the west side of the greenhouse to block the sun and excess light into the structure. During the winter, the trees shed off the leaves, allowing the extra sun to get into the greenhouse.

Alternatively, you can install roll-up shades. Roll-up shades are closed during the summer to protect the plants from the sun and remain open in winter to allow more sun and light to enter.

Heating and Ventilation Problems

Greenhouses provide a temperature-controlled environment to meet the needs of your plants. You need to maintain the heating and ventilation equipment and ensure they're working properly. Check the equipment regularly and do full maintenance on them before the winter growing season.

If there are gaps in the greenhouse exterior, you can use new glass panes to fill out the large holes or caulk to fill small holes in the exterior. This ensures heat you maintain heat inside the greenhouse.

Paint all walls black, as doing so makes sure that you attract and retain more heat.

You can install roof vents between the ceiling and the rooftop. In most greenhouses, hot air is always trapped at the top of the ceiling and prevents the crops from receiving enough warmth. Installing vents can easily push away hot air and allow fresh air from the outside, thus increasing fresh air circulation.

You can also use fans installed diagonally at the opposite corners of the greenhouse, which increases fresh air circulation inside. Switch off the fans in the winter to conserve heat.

You should also consider a watering system or piping system. Make sure you properly install the water system and that it works as desired. You must also do frequent maintenance on the pipes to ensure no leaks.

Weed Control

Weeds growing in the greenhouses and other covered structures are among the most persistent problems that many farmers face. These weeds affect plants' quality, and other types of weeds can act as hosts for pests like whiteflies, snails, mites, and slugs.

Weeds that grow under the benches inside the greenhouse will usually host some pests and fungi; therefore, you need to develop mechanisms to control the weed growth.

Removing the weed from the greenhouse benches, pots, and even the floor is important in managing the greenhouse and maintaining its aesthetic. A ground cloth put under the benches is highly recommended for weed management.

An accumulation of potting media on the ground can appear to act as the perfect environment for weed growth if you do not collect it. A ground cloth can easily collect the spilled potting media and prevent any germination of weed seeds.

Weeds that have already grown under the benches may force you to use herbicide to help manage them. There is a wide variety of herbicides in the market, but most are for outdoor use, while very few are for indoor use. Don't be tempted to buy the ones labeled for use outdoors, as it may have negative effects on the crops grown inside. In extreme cases, it can affect your plants in the season. Vapor from some of the traditional herbicides can be trapped inside the structure and will not only affect the crops, but they could also be a health hazard to the people working in the greenhouse.

When applying greenhouse herbicides on the benches, read the instructions carefully. There are two types of herbicides in the greenhouse: Pre-emergence activity and Marengo. You can apply the herbicide labeled "pre-emergency activity" when the crop is present, and you can water the plant pot even after application. You should not apply barespot herbicides on the pot.

You cannot use Marengo herbicide when the plant is present; instead, apply Marengo herbicide before the start of the growing season. Watering the area with the applied herbicide activates its residual compound, which can damage plants in the area due to volatilization from the herbicide.

Weed Management

Managing the weed growing conditions is essential for every greenhouse. A weed-free environment reduces the need for pesticides and increases the production of high-quality crops. Proper weed control practices help keep pests, insects, and weed diseases at bay.

Weeds compete with your crops for light, water, and nutrients; therefore, you should remove them as soon as possible before they affect your crops' growth. These weeds carry their own viruses too, which can damage or infect your crops.

A weed management program will help you to manage and control the weeds in your greenhouse effectively while helping you come up with control measures.

Sources of Weed Seeds

Weeds come from a variety of sources, some of which include:

- Ventilation fans blow weed seeds from outside into the greenhouse.
- Contaminated seeds.
- Infected plants are transplanted in the greenhouse from an external source.
- Poor plant growing area and storage or using dirty pots and containers.
- Contaminated or uncovered soil from under tables and benches.
- From the irrigation systems and water ponds.

CHAPTER 14:

Mistakes To Avoid

IN fact, truth to tell, many gardeners continue to make mistakes despite having acquired years of experience. The most common reason why mistakes are made in ignorance. Some people simply think that if they can raise carrots, then they can raise lettuce, or if they can grow an orange tree, then they understand how to take care of mint. This attitude ignores the subtle (and not so subtle) differences between plants, and simply reduces a vast topic into too rigid a formula. When this happens, dead plants and poor harvests are prone to follow. By being aware of these mistakes, you reduce your level of ignorance, and you increase your chances of avoiding them yourself. In the world of growing, much as with life in general, we are required to act on our knowledge if we want to see the best results.

Not Doing Your Research

We've looked at a handful of plants throughout this book, and, while some of them share similarities (such as thyme and rosemary), they all have notable differences in how much light, water, fertilizer, space, and humidity they want, as well as which nutrients they like best, and what ph level they require to stay healthy. If there can be this much of a difference between the small handful that we were able to look at, then you can only imagine how much variety there is across the plant kingdom. Not only that, but keep in mind that different subspecies of plants often have their own preferences that, while similar to each other, can show a great deal of variation.

Instead, do your research on your plants. If you are not very technologically savvy, then you should consider stopping in at your local gardening center and asking them for advice. The chances are good, you were going to get your seeds from them anyway, so why not pick their brains first to find out everything you need to know. Questions you should consider asking first are: How often should I water this plant? What type of fertilizer do they need, and how often do they need it? Does it take long to germinate? How long does it take to grow? When can I expect it to start fruiting? How much light does it want? Does it prefer direct sunlight or partial shade? What temperature should it be kept at? How much humidity does it require? What ph level will it need? Is there anything I should know about pollinating it by hand?

Asking questions and doing your research should be the very first step you take when considering growing something that is new to you. Before you, even look up the price of seeds or seedlings, ask all the questions you need answering, whether or not you are capable of providing an ideal environment for this type of plant. Being prepared with information will save you money as you can avoid those that are not a good fit, and you will also spare yourself the disappointment of watching a new plant wilt and die.

Growing Too Much at Once

When they are beginning, many people have big, grand plans for their indoor gardens. They are going to have lettuce and tomatoes, carrots and eggplants, a peach tree, some rosemary, and a bunch of mints. In theory, this sounds amazing. Who wouldn't want to have that much delicious food at their fingertips? But in practice, this is often a recipe for disaster.

The first issue that many people are going to run into by expanding too fast is the fact that things are not growing as they thought. Just because you plant a seed, does not mean it is going to grow. It can be particularly discouraging for new gardeners when it happens once but consider when it happens to several plants all at the same time. Furthermore, even if they do germinate, each plant is going to grow at a different rate, and this means that you will need to balance the needs of several different plants that are all at various stages of development. Observe the use of the word "balance." Gardening takes up your time and attention; you need to watch your plants to get a sense of how they are doing, and then adjust their care accordingly. While you might think that this will be quick and easy, many new gardeners are completely shocked at just how long this can take.

When you are starting, begin small and then expand as you become more comfortable with looking after a garden. While I would suggest starting with a single plant, many will find this to be too small to make it worth their time. If you need more, allow yourself 2–3 plants but limit yourself to this. Pick plants that have similar care routines and environmental requirements so that you can worry about building one environment, rather than fine-tuning several. Take these plants through to harvest before you add any more. That way, you know what is required for each step.

In the care process. Start slow, and add more as your skill and understanding increase. Approach it with a sensible attitude. Looking at this way, becoming proficient at gardening is not that different from any other skill.

Planting Seeds Too Close Together

When you are first putting seeds (or even seedlings) into a container, it will seem like space is abundant. After all, seeds are super-tiny, and so you can put a whole whack of them in a container without it feeling like they are crowding each other out. While this is true at these early stages of growth, you will quickly come to regret this decision when your plants start to grow, and you realize that they have no space at all.

First off, while you will notice the lack of space on top of the soil, it is really what is happening under the soil that is damaging your plants the most. Their roots are going to start to get tangled and fight to find their own space while they grow, and this is going to cause several issues that negatively affect their overall health. Those same roots are going to have to compete with each other for nutrients, and this means that all of your plants are going to be far less healthy when compared to those that get all the nutrients they need without a struggle. The struggle to fight for nutrients wastes energy, energy which would be better utilized in promoting growth. Stunted plants are one such result of being planted too close together.

Another factor to bear in mind is that pests and diseases can much more easily spread from plant to plant when they are too close together. Moreover, they have more places to hide; it is much harder to see all the nooks and crannies of your plants when they obscure each other. Therefore, it is evident that planting too close together creates more difficulties with pests and diseases and smaller harvests of less tasty food.

Not Checking for Pests or Cleaning for Disease

Speaking of pests—have you been checking for them? If not, then how do you know that your plants are still healthy? Just because you do not see pests when you look at your plants does not mean that they might not already be feeding off your plants. There are many telltale signs of infection, such as discoloration in leaves, bumps or holes in the leaves, or leaves that have begun to wilt for no discernible reason. The longer an infestation takes hold, the more damage your plants will sustain.

You want to ensure your plants are free of infestation or infection; the simplest precaution is to check them daily. This takes up time, that resource many new growers discount when they decide to grow too many plants. While many pests can be detected on sight, there are more than a few that either hide or are invisible to the naked eye. If you see pests, you need to start treating your plants immediately. But you should also do spot tests daily to see if any such parasites are hiding. Use your rake to check the soil at the roots, as many pests lay eggs in the soil; the offspring of these eggs will, given the chance, chew away at the stem. If the paper comes away with streaks of blood, then there are pests you are going to have to deal with. There are many ways of dealing with pests, but you should do your research before embarking on any of them. Since fruits, vegetables, and herbs are all plants that we grow with the intention of eating, it is crucial to ensure that whatever pesticide or solution you use to treat your plants is not going to harm the food you eat.

While you are making it a habit to check for pests, you should also keep your eyes open for signs of disease. White powdery mildew, molds, discoloration, wilting branches, rotting fruit—all of these are signs that your plants have caught a disease. The first step in tackling most sicknesses is to cut away any infected parts and immediately dispose of them outdoors. Apply treatments to your plants after ensuring those treatments are not harmful to humans.

Next, check the ph level of your soil to make sure that they have enough nutrients, as too few can leave them sickly, and too many can cause a nutrient burn. Finally, though just as importantly, make sure that dead plant matter is removed from the area. The compost that is used in the soil is fine, but leaves or branches that have fallen off the plants and are rotting in the general area are quite harmful. This rotting plant matter, when it is not being used as part of a properly planned feeding system, can introduce harmful bacteria to your growing area. Always make sure you remove any dead or fallen plant matter from the growing area and wash your hands first before you start handling your plants.

Conclusion

Greenhouse is a must-have for any gardener. It has so many potentials uses and makes your life so much easier than you will wonder how you ever managed without one. You can spend as much, or as little, money as you want on your greenhouse, it depends on your budget. However, what is important is that you choose the site and then prepare it properly. Doing so will reduce the amount of maintenance you need to do and extend the lifespan of your greenhouse.

Your greenhouse needs to be secure against the wind and any potential damage from the surroundings, think footballs and falling branches. Set up properly, it will be very low maintenance and an absolute pleasure to grow in.

You can extend your growing season, being able to start your seeds off earlier in the year and grow delicate crops longer into the cooler months. For anyone outside of the warmest areas, it is essential as it will make the difference when it comes to getting your crops to produce a viable harvest.

This book has tried to answer all of your potential questions and show you the many benefits of a greenhouse. With everything you have learned in this book, you will now be able to set up your greenhouse and manage it easily. It will reduce the amount of work you need to do and allow you to grow plants that would otherwise have been out of your reach.

You do have to remember that greenhouses come with their own potential set of problems. However, most of these can be avoided purely by ensuring there is suitable ventilation and air circulation. These two issues are by far the number one cause of problems within any glasshouse.

Pollination can be an issue, but leaving vents open will allow pollinating insects in, and, as you learned earlier, you can always pollinate your plants by hand.

It is vital that you either have a suitable irrigation system in your greenhouse or that you water your plants regularly. On hotter days, they will require daily watering, particularly if they are in smaller containers. Lack of water causes leaf, flower, and fruit drop, which will impact your potential harvest.

If you are planning on putting a greenhouse in your garden or on your allotment, then I'd recommend you go and size it up. Look for a suitable space and measure it up to determine what size greenhouse you can put in. You may decide to start with a portable greenhouse or a hoop house, depending on the space and budget available to you.

Making the decisions about the type of floor and foundation need to be made right at the start as these are very difficult, and expensive, to change later on. I wouldn't recommend growing directly in the soil as it will quickly become a burden and turn your greenhouse into a chore.

I will guarantee that in your first year, you will overcrowd your greenhouse in your excitement. By the second, you will want another greenhouse or a bigger one as you understand the benefits and how great a greenhouse is. I can see so many benefits, and after a couple of poor growing years, this will make a massive difference to my ability to produce the more delicate crops I like.

Owning a greenhouse is a lot of fun and full of potential. I would highly recommend you get one, as large as you can afford and fit in. You will enjoy it immensely as it allows you to grow successfully a wide variety of crops that you would otherwise have struggled to grow. These useful glasshouses are well worth the investment and will give you years of enjoyment and growing pleasure.

www.ingramcontent.com/pod-product-compliance
Lightning Source LLC
Chambersburg PA
CBHW081402070526
44583CB00020B/2645